Leaving The Military
Life After Resettlement:
How to Get a New Job That Doesn't Suck

Chris Hitchens

DEDICATION

To Judith, James and Will

My three best friends in the world

X

CONTENTS

ACKNOWLEDGMENTS

There are far too many people to mention.

But to everyone that has contributed
to the creation of this book,
both consciously and unconsciously,
both good and bad over the years

Thank you.
You taught me what I know today.

HOW TO READ THIS BOOK

Ok, so I know you know how to read, but I wanted to make this book as squaddie proof as possible! So, I have added a short explanation regarding the structure of this book and how to best use it to help you.

Chapters

I have written the chapters covering key points, and these can be found in the table of contents for ease of navigation. You will notice that I explain key exercises and tasks for you to do throughout the chapters. Fear not, I have captured these at the end of every chapter in a conclusion called Action Plan.

Your Next Plan of Action

This is the collection of the exercises mentioned throughout the chapters that will help you. Have a go at these. If you need further help or the resources mentioned in the book, you can find these on the website: www.leavingthemilitary.co.uk

Action Points

During some of the chapters, I have added action points to point out when you need to do something. Add these to your to-do list.

The Website

http://www.leavingthemilitary.co.uk
The website gets mentioned throughout the book. Here, you can access a secure environment where there are:

Resources

Spreadsheets and documents to help you complete the exercises in this book.

Discussion Forums

A place for you, me and other readers to connect and discuss the points in this book if you need extra clarity.

Publications

A link to the other books I have written. This book is an overview of the leaving process. I am in the process of writing books to supplement this book, where I can focus on one particular aspect and go far deeper.

Contact me

You will be able to contact me, and while I hope you take the time to post a positive review on Amazon or iTunes, it's always nice to hear from people after they have read my book (even if it is to say it was 'soft, strong and very absorbent'...!) I am always looking to improve my books, so welcome any feedback so I can help you get ahead.

INTRODUCTION

I was a Gazelle Pilot in the Army Air Corps and served for just under 14 years; if Carlsberg did jobs, eh? I remember one of my instructors saying to me, "One day, you'll get out of bed, and you won't want to fly anymore." I remember thinking in absolute disbelief that day would never come as I loved flying!

However, that day came for me, like it does everyone. It wasn't long after 9/11; I had spent three years of bliss flying a gazelle helicopter around Cyprus and then was posted back to Northern Ireland. My first day in the Squadron hit me like a ton of bricks, and I knew after three previous years in Northern Ireland that I was done. That was me, I wanted to leave.

I remember telling the boss that I wanted to leave the Army. No one was particularly happy with my decision. My family thought I was nuts, the Army was characteristically unsympathetic (as they were back then) and I was filled with a mixture of emotions; fear, trepidation, excitement, anxiety, sadness, happiness and much more.

I felt like it was me against the world because there was a growing queue of people lining up to tell me that I was making a huge mistake and that I was giving up a great job and opportunity not many people get.

So, like me back then, here you are. Maybe you're thinking of leaving the forces, or have already decided and are now in the process of leaving and feel like you are in an emotional washing machine! Don't worry, you are not the only one and hopefully, through telling my story, what I learnt, the mistakes I made (and the bits of luck I had!) you can make the most of the time you have left and plan accordingly.

Who is This Book For?

This book can help anyone who wants to change career. Especially if you work for an institution, be you a policeman, fireman, stripper at Spearmint Rhino, or politician (the last two can be interchangeable).

However, I have written this book based on my experiences of leaving the British military, and it's for anyone who served in the British Army, Air Force, or Navy. It isn't necessarily aimed at those with a commission, or even for the private soldier. It's for everyone. It's primarily themed for those who are in the process of leaving but can act as a good aide-memoire to those who left years ago.

I'm hoping that my journey and experiences can help *you*.

Since leaving, I've had permanent jobs, been fired, made redundant, have worked as a limited company contractor, I've set up my own businesses, one failed and one went global, and I've had time not working in-between. But they all had one thing in common - the feeling of uncertainty of whether I'm compatible with the civilian working world. A question which I'm still answering on a daily basis!

One thing I can guarantee is that making that transition will be hard, but not impossible.

There are many pitfalls, and civvy street has its own ways of doing things. Which, chances are, you won't be familiar with or might have changed while you have been working for her majesty. It's easy to make mistakes when you leave things down to your good looks, killer wit and propensity to lose all your clothes at a rugby match when someone shouts "Naked Bar". Knowledge is power, and you need a plan.

The areas I am focusing on in this book are:
- How you feel leaving the military - getting you ready for the mental shift
- Who YOU are, and how you want to spend the rest of your days
- Keeping you on track – your Accountability Group
- Finding out what job you will succeed in
- Getting you ready for your new career
- Getting your CV ready for your new career
- The interview
- The salary negotiation
- The offer process
- Becoming a contractor

- Setting up your own business

I plan on writing other books where I will go into much more detail on each subject. But this first one is a general view of the process and what to expect. A brief overview, if you like. If, as you go through the book, you find you need to visit an area in more detail, there will be a more in-depth book to help you. Visit www.leavingthemilitary.co.uk for more details. You can ask questions on the website, or get in touch with me via the website. I would love to hear from you.

What I can tell you is that everything about your life is about to change. Although you could argue that life and work are bound together for lots of people, like emergency services workers, there are few situations where you live, breathe, and eat the job in the same way as being in the military.

The first thing to do is come to terms with the change.

1 SO HOW DO YOU REALLY FEEL ABOUT LEAVING THE MILITARY?

If your response is anything other than "gutted", you're already part of the way to accepting your future and planning your own personal 'what next'. With resources being somewhat stretched for the forces in recent years, there may be part of you that feels relieved that you won't have to deal with the stress of 'all work and no play', any longer. Especially if it has taken you away from your loved ones at times. If you're a workaholic, then you're probably already thinking about a challenge that can – and will – take up every minute of the day, seven days a week.

Unless you already have something in mind that creates a 'family firm', with your partner or spouse working alongside you, you might also want to appreciate this as a chance to look again at who you are, and why you work to live rather than live to work. The big question is (and it's not an easy one to answer), what do you want out of life?

If you're planning on setting up your own business, keep an eye out, as I will be publishing a book specifically aimed at this to help you navigate through the pitfalls.

So, how are you planning to spend your time to make sure that you still have that all important 'sense of purpose' that will leave both your sense of being and your bank account fulfilled?

The Five Stages of Grief
First, let's talk about the Five Stages of Grief, written by David Kessler and Elisabeth Kübler-Ross. People think about grief in terms of bereavement or the end of a relationship, but it's just as relevant to leaving a long-term career or experiencing a huge life change.

In project management terms, this is referred to as 'The Change Curve'. This relates to how people react to change when an organisation delivers a large project. In short, people don't like change (ironically, project managers are great at forcing it on other people, but hate it when it happens to them!).

The same could be said for most of my readers who have served in the military. You have delivered more change than you know all over the world, in under-resourced circumstances, sometimes in a one-way firing range, with the indigenous population not very happy that you are there, and often in a very ambiguous environment.

But all said, no matter what part you played, you experienced change. Now it's going to happen to not just you, but your nearest and dearest as well and in quite a radical way.

So now you are faced with the possibility of going through all the five stages of grief. You may be lucky and only experience one, or maybe two stages. None the less, this is as relevant to you and your family as anyone else going through a life-change such as leaving the military or re-entering the workforce after a long period of absence.

The Stages
Denial – this is the one that keeps you (relatively) sane when the bomb first drops. The numbness and bewilderment stop the feelings rushing in and completely overwhelming us, and we just about manage to blunder through. However, sooner or later, you'll start to accept the reality that you've lost something central to your life, and that's where the next stage comes in.

Anger – this is the "why me, what have I done to deserve this" stage and varies from person to person whether it's specific or generalised. You might blame the military, you might blame yourself, you might blame something else altogether. The trick is to start channelling that anger into action, even if that action is only getting yourself together enough to start making plans.

Bargaining – if you haven't done a bit of "if you let me stay, I'll never dodge a Christmas Guard duty ever again", you're probably just not at the bargaining stage yet. The bargaining stage of grief tends to wind itself through all the others and even has a tendency to jump up and take us by surprise when we think we're completely over something.

Depression – if you're starting to feel empty and hopeless about your massive change in circumstances, then this is where you are. We all go through this, where all of a sudden life looks like climbing Everest and you literally have no idea where to start and all you want is your Mum. It can be an overwhelming thought and all of a sudden you start to doubt yourself and then feel terrible! My advice is to stay off the booze and go for a walk and listen to audiobooks that will rub off on you and get you back into the right frame of mind. Having been in this place, I recommend my top five reads on the website: www.leavingthemilitary.co.uk.

This phase is painful but isn't going to last forever, and it's a perfectly appropriate response to losing such a huge part of your life. Remember, asking for help is a sign of strength. Suffering through in silence is a sign of weakness. The trick is to use that emptiness. Don't deny you're going through it, as it's a necessary step in getting out the other side.

Acceptance – this doesn't mean you're okay, it just means that you're in a position to act, you have come to terms with reality, you have a plan. You have accepted you have a 'new normal'. You've processed what's going on, and rather than just letting it happen to you, you're engaging with it and taking action. You realise the light at the end of a tunnel is not an on-coming train!

The best way to get through the five stages is to form a plan. And do it one small bit at a time. There is a well-known saying to help you approach the planning stage: Anyone can eat an elephant, you just do it one mouthful at a time!

So, if your circumstances and fears look about the size and weight as something that has big floppy grey ears, tusks and just simply refuses to let you forget, then it's time to start taking it one bite at a time. No need to bite off more than you can chew, just one mouthful at a time and we will get there. I hate clichés like the plague, but you get my meaning.

Remember, this is character building stuff, right? So of course, the five stages of grief don't necessarily happen in any kind of set order for everyone, and you might even find yourself swinging between all of them in the space of an hour, then landing right back at the beginning again.

It's not unusual for two or three to show up at the same time – denial, anger and bargaining are famous for this. These are completely human feelings, we all feel like this, so you're not alone. Now that you know that what you are feeling is completely normal for our species (even though I admit, it feels far from normal), you have the tools in this book at your disposal to help you get through the dark bits. If you are struggling, get yourself onto www.leavingthemilitary.co.uk and the discussion forums. The people there can help you through.

Silence is a sign of weakness and asking for help is a sign of your strength of character. So take your cape off, this is not the resistance to interrogation phase, and admit that you're human if you need help.

So now that you know where you are on the rollercoaster which is the 5 stages of grief, in the next part, we can investigate what makes you tick and work out what your starting point is.

What follows – and what follows at the end of every chapter – is a plan. A few short exercises that will help you get your thoughts in order, and see a way forward.

So get yourself a brew and strap yourself in while I hurl some good old well-worn military motivational phrases to get you inspired. Work hard, you are in your own time now ladies and gentlemen ☺

The 'What Do I Want to Do with My Life' Exercise

Serious question - when was the last time you sat down and had to evaluate who you were? One of the first exercises I did was the 'what do I want to do with my life' exercise.

Basically, I got a piece of A4 paper, I drew a line through the middle and then down the centre to give myself four boxes:

1. What was I good at?
2. What was I not good at?
3. What did I enjoy doing?
4. What did I not enjoy doing?

I worked on this for about a month and promised myself to take 10 minutes a day to look at it and work on it. Whenever I wrote something I would ask 'Why?' and 'So what?' and would keep asking that till I could get down to the root cause, the essence of what made me tick. I have added this to the action plan at the end of the chapter, but if like me you are massively impatient then try it yourself now. You might be surprised at what it throws up.

Getting to the Good Stuff – The Five Why's?

One of the best ways to find out what motivates you and what doesn't is to use this well-known 'Root Cause Analysis' project management technique called 'The Five Whys'. Basically, if you ask 'why' five times, you should be able to boil absolutely anything down to its base-answer, otherwise known as the root cause.

Let's think about how this works with a fairly simple issue that can be misdiagnosed: if your nose is running, the answer is not to wipe it on your sweat-shirt, or designer jumper knotted around the neck in a gentlemanly fashion (if you are of the commissioned variety). This will only address a symptom (and according to my five-year-old is a totally acceptable form of resolution, especially if I have a sleeve that is accessible). We need to ask why you have a runny nose, and keep asking why until we find the underlying problem.

You don't need to watch the medical drama House box-set to work out that you actually need a couple of days in bed, some vitamin C and a heavy dose of Netflix (and possibly a knighthood if it's man-flu).

In essence, we have ignored the noise and distractions surrounding the problem, and we have solved the problem causing the symptoms. Not the other way around, which is what a lot of people do when they are in a hurry, or misidentify the symptom as a problem. This is because they only ever see the noise and distractions and are sometimes ignorant of the underlying problems. They then wonder why their life feels like a knife fight in a phone box.

Take the time to do this exercise properly and keep asking why. Get to the root cause. The root cause is your foundation that you build your plan on.

What I want you to do now is look at your 'What Do I Want To Do With My Life' Exercise. It's time to examine every point you have written down and ask why 5 times. Try and get to the root cause because you may have written down a mere symptom and not uncovered the good stuff. This bit requires complete honesty and for you to keep coming back to it until you have completed it.

A good way if you are busy is to do 10 minutes in the morning and 20 minutes at night, rather than trying to complete it in one sitting. Remember, anyone can eat an elephant, you just need to do it in bite-sized chunks.

If you are really struggling, the next section will help you complete this exercise.

Keeping You on Track – Form an Accountability Group
You're probably sat there asking 'why' 5 times thinking, this is boring and hard work. Unfortunately, some of the richest people in the world are rich because they realised that getting the boring stuff correct and addressing the mundane tasks is the key.

It's very rare that the shiny, sexy tasks alone get you where you need to be. So this next bit is about keeping you on the straight and narrow when your enthusiasm goes AWOL (Absent Without Leave for all you readers who used to take apples in for your teachers every day!).

If like me you struggle with this kind of thing because it feels a bit happy-clappy, then employ your nearest and dearest to form what is known as an Accountability Group.

This is a group of people that will keep you focused and ensure that you keep to your timeline. This is important, because you will have down-days, and for some people leaving the military, these can quite easily become down-weeks, and God forbid, down months. There are way too many homeless ex-service people, and I don't want you to become another one, so get people to hold you to account! This is a massively important foundation to your plan.

One very important thing to point out is that an Accountability Group is a two-way deal. Your Accountability Group needs to know what their purpose is, and that this is serious stuff. This is definitely not a favour or an informal chat. This is for someone who is invested in your future. This should be a diarised weekly meeting with a hard-set agenda that you cannot waffle your way out of with a sick note.

Equally, the members of your Accountability Group need to commit to the process. If you want to do this properly, and I thoroughly recommend this, then write up some 'Terms of Reference' together. To help, I have put a template on my website www.leavingthemilitary.co.uk in the reference section. This will keep you both honest and won't let you shirk your mutual responsibilities when it gets tough and life gets in the way – and life will get in the way. This serves as a useful hand-rail to keep you on track and won't let tasks drift.

For my Accountability Group, I had to report to my fiancée every week with what I had achieved against what I said I would do. This Accountability Group made me tackle the hard and boring tasks, and she challenged me on tasks that I hadn't even thought of – why would I? I was still thinking like a soldier. Also, we made sure there were both positive and negative consequences to keep me incentivised. So as well as not letting her down, it meant there was an upside when I delivered my promises.

Get your Accountability Group to challenge you every week and push you to think through the hard stuff. It's even better if you have a civilian friend who has a similar role to the one you are hoping to transition into. They will be able to help steer you. Even more useful is if you have an ex-colleague who is a year or more on from leaving the military themselves. They've got the t-shirt. Why try to reinvent the wheel?

To this day, I still do the 'what do I want to do with my life' exercise, and it's still a hard task and no easier, and rightly so! Personally, I know what I want to do with my life and what gives me that sense of purpose, that sense of mission that drives me. That's the important bit: defining your sense of purpose. And that's exactly what this book is about.

Once you have your accountability group in place to help you, you will be gob-smacked that you never did it before and even more gob-smacked when you observe other people just drifting through life complaining.

These drifters are not stupid people, they know far more trigonometry than me and can probably spell 'neckasery' properly, but yet they have no idea why they are here and what makes them tick. They are just waiting for retirement, where ironically, they will have much more time to think about the time they have wasted not having a defined purpose that makes them truly happy. I know this sounds evangelical, but when you nail your 'why', your sense of purpose, it is a personal epiphany.

You read any great leader's book and you'll learn they all have mentors to help them. As they say, every master was once a disaster. They stay in their current state because they are mindful of their accountabilities and it keeps them focused. This can help you too, and it costs nothing, so get on with it!

Finding your purpose in life is not always as easy as you might think – how many things do you do out of duty or habit, and yet when you analyse your feelings, find that you're at best neutral, and at worst resentful of the time they take up in your life? Wouldn't it be great if you could get out of bed every morning and feel excited and actually driven by your sense of purpose?

I know this all sounds a bit new age, but you have a wonderful opportunity in front of you to re-define yourself – make the most of it.

So now you have done your 'what do I want to do with my life' exercise and have examined each point by asking why five times, you and your Accountability Group should have a pretty good idea what makes you tick and what excites you.

Well done you, you are a step further than 90% of other people. Most people have no real idea what makes them happy and what doesn't. Most people have a vague idea at best. You are now in a great place to start shaping your future to achieve the things that will give you that important sense of purpose.

Dos & Don'ts for Your Accountability Group
- DO support, but DON'T try to fix
- DO help work through feelings, DON'T set deadlines for those feelings to 'go'
- DO recognise the loss, DON'T minimise it
- DO admit defeat if professional help is required, DON'T bury your head in the sand

Time for Your Personal Strategy
Strategy is one of those words that strikes fear into most people, me included. You don't have to be sitting in a leather chair stroking a white cat or be a chess grandmaster. What strategy simply means to me is:

Why do I want to do something? What is my plan to get to a specific outcome and how am I going to achieve this with the resources I have available?

No doubt people will have their own views, but to keep it simple and by the way, strategy should always be simple, this is my starting point.

My advice with any strategy is to start at the end and work backwards. Where is this all leading to? What is your version of utopia? When you're old and surrounded by your family and the lights are going out, what did you want the purpose of your life to be? What legacy do you want to leave behind? Let's work back from that.

A great casing point is John F Kennedy. He stood up in 1962 and said, "By the end of the decade, we will send a man to the moon AND bring him back safely."

This came as a bit of a shock to the boys and girls at NASA. But what JFK did was set out the outcome that he wanted. He wanted the USA to win the space race. He and everyone else had no idea how they would achieve this, but he gave them a simple endgame and had the authority to give them the resources. His statement was one that everyone could visualise, and because it was simple it inspired people into 'why' they needed to achieve this. He started at the end, painted an inspiring image in people's mind and gave them the space to get on with it (excuse the pun!).

Help Finding Your 'Why'

Your 'why' is one of the most important parts of your strategy. We will cover this throughout the book, and I will be as monotonous as possible (and on purpose!) to always try to get you to ask that question to yourself at least five times, so we can get to the root cause of what makes you tick.

So, to help you maintain your momentum and keep you going through the low points (and you will have them, we all do), it's worth asking your Accountability Group of trusted friends what they think your strengths are, as it's easy to be clouded about those too. Remember, one of the rules of your Accountability Group is they have to be 100% honest with you, no matter how scathing.

We all think we're the karaoke king after a few beers inside us (actually, I am - ask my deaf neighbours!). Try making your own list; keep it to yourself until you have compared it to what your friends and colleagues have to say. Also, don't worry if those qualities don't automatically look like they would be any use in the workplace; a "good mate" translates as a team player who is considerate of their colleagues, for example.

This exercise will lead you to a core piece of information that will help you massively - your personal values. Most people don't know what these are and it's astounding when you can pinpoint your own values – what means the most to you?

It's so important to have a vision of who you want to be as a person. When you come to terms with leaving the military and are clear on your values and your vision for who you want to be, you will no longer be defined by a rank, a uniform or a stereotype.

You may have got to this point and are wondering what my 'why' is. If that is the case, then I'm happy to let you into a secret. You're reading my 'why'.

My 'why' is that I get a massive sense of achievement from helping people by sharing valuable knowledge and an even bigger kick when they succeed, knowing that I had a small part to play in helping someone live life by their rules. That's my why.

You might be thinking that this is a load of rubbish and that I am doing it for the money. If that was the case, I would be charging 10 times more for this book. Money is circumstance, a by-product of your 'why'. Money just creates opportunities – which in turn may or may not create happiness. But when it comes to creating opportunities, money doesn't even come close to creating opportunities like knowledge does.

Positive Mental Attitude

I am going to place a couple of spoilers here if you are an avid reader. But hopefully, this will help you big time. I listen to audiobooks a lot, especially when I'm travelling. I listen to them on 2x speed so I can get through them in half the time. Now there's a real productivity hack for you. I really enjoy learning stuff from other successful people and what I have learnt is that Henry Ford was bang on the money:

Whether you think you can, or you think you can't...You're probably right.

Anthony Robbins, the self-help guru, Napoleon Hill, author of Think and Grow Rich, and a raft of other successful people all agree with visualising yourself having already achieved your goal. If you want to be a billionaire, tell yourself you are already one and act like it. If it's scoring a goal, then visualise the ball in the back of the net. 80% of success is adopting the right mindset. If you didn't know, this is called 'autosuggestion' which basically means 'the hypnotic or subconscious adoption of an idea which one has originated oneself'.

This is such a powerful tool, and as we are now at the end of the first chapter I want you to look at the thoughts you have captured on paper and the ideas you've worked with your friends and family and your Accountability Group to shape your future. Now smile, think positive. You're at the start of a great journey, and you are making positive steps.

Well done! Have a short holiday... there, how was it?

THIS CHAPTER IN A NUTSHELL

Your Plan of Action
- Note where you are in the five stages of grief.
- Make notes on what matters to you.
- Do the 'what do I want to do with my life' exercise.
- Go through every point and ask 'why' five times to get to the root cause.
- Get an Accountability Group to report into. These will keep you honest, motivated and will help you get over the emotional humps!
- Write a 'terms of reference' for your Accountability Group (get the template on the website).
- Ask your Accountability Group to do the 'what do I want to with my life' exercise. Compare notes and get them to help you with the five whys.
- Get in touch with ex-colleagues who have been out of the services for a year or more. Ask for their advice!
- Collate all of the above and visualise the outcome you want. What is your end game?
- Smile and get that positive attitude, spread it around and remember what Henry Ford said...
- Pat yourself on the back and write to me on the website to share where you are on your journey. I would love to hear from you.

Things To Note
- Remember, anyone can eat an elephant... Just do it one mouthful at a time.
- Concentrate on the problem, not the symptom.
- Do not get consumed with the noise. This is just a distraction.
- Asking for help is a sign of strength. Staying silent is a sign of weakness
- Get onto the website www.leavingthemilitary.co.uk if you need help or clarity on any of the points in this chapter.

2 LIFE AND OTHER STUFF

It's Not All About You

If you're single, you might want to skip this part. Although if you're leaving the army through choice because you want to settle down and call somewhere home, read on.

You might have spent the last few pages thinking what you want from your life, and what you want to do next. But this is going to have a massive impact on your family too, not least on where you live in terms of work, schools, facilities, and your wider social circle outside the military.

They need to be part of this discussion. For example, are the kids going to go to a day school, or will they be at the very least weekly boarders? Might they even be home-schooled? Where are they regarding crucial exams? Will they be joining a school in the middle of the school year, or even in the middle of a term? What does your partner do? Are they using this opportunity to think about a career change themselves, or perhaps even study for additional qualifications? Might this be something you want or need to do?

The questions all tend to be ones that spawn several more questions, then breed again and create even more. For example, here's just a small checklist of things that will affect the family:

- Where to live, and whether to rent or buy
- Finding a school (or schools, if they fall into several year groups) for the children
- Registering with a GP/Dentist/Optician
- How transport links affect work/school travel

They will all impact on what kind of salary you need to be looking for, as the ideal location for all of you will be at a premium, with good schools, good transport links, and good health facilities. Up until now, you've had these provided to you on a plate.

To help you answer these important questions, I have compiled a list on the 'logistics spreadsheet' on the website www.leavingthemilitary.co.uk This will help you plan the tasks that you need to consider and work through before leaving.

It may also be a good idea to get your nearest and dearest to do the 'what do I want to do with my life' exercise. That way you can compare your aspirations.

Where Do I Live and What Do I Earn?

This next exercise is a fun one, and will probably give you the biggest headache. However, it's one of the most crucial steps, and will also help to determine what you do and where you live. Your salary isn't just a question of what you'd like to earn, it's what you will need to earn, especially if you have a specific area of the country in mind that also happens to be a big city or a thriving commuter belt.

It will also give you the tools you need for salary negotiation. Up until now, your salary has been dependent on your rank and years of service, and has included a lot of extras that you won't find in civilian life. If you're not careful, that will lead to you accepting what sounds like a reasonable salary and finding yourself struggling each month and unable to support your family properly.

Set yourself up a spreadsheet and work out what your monthly expenses are likely to be. I've made a spreadsheet you can download from the www.leavingthemilitary.co.uk website. In the most basic terms, these expenses are:

- Your living expenses – including rent or mortgage, utilities including gas, electricity and water rates, council tax, television licence (or cable/satellite subscription), and food bills (estimate this at around £15 per person per day – and the food is going up in price all the time).
- Communication expenses – landline, mobile phone bills and internet.
- Debt – loan repayments (if you have them), car payments, credit card payments, any other loan or hire-purchase agreements. It's better to over rather than underestimate these.

- Insurance – if you have a family, this is crucial; over and above any car, home and contents insurance, you should at the very least have a life policy, and consider both health and income protection policies as well. If you are over 50, start a funeral plan – the average costs of no-frills funerals in the UK as of 2017 is around £4,136 for a traditional burial, and £3,214 for cremation. That's a huge lump sum to find when you least want to worry about debt.
- Entertainment – if you don't factor in money for fun, life is going to be very stressful and dull. Calculate a sum for a family holiday each year, a few weekend trips, shopping trips over and above the basics, eating out as a family (and as a couple) at least once a month, and any other trips such as theatre, sports events, cinema, and festivals. Gym membership should probably go in here too, although you may wish to consider that an essential living expense (it's likely to cancel itself out in discounts on your health and life insurance premiums for a start).
- A pension - you may think that your military pension is going to keep you in a lifestyle that you're used to. But frankly speaking, I would say that 80% of people are in for a shock. My advice here is interviewing at least three independent financial advisors and getting them to appraise your pension and take you through what they can offer. Do not go to the bank for this as they can only offer you the bank's products and they will be less than competitive.

However much time you've got before you leave the military, the time to start building a cash buffer for emergencies is now. If you don't already have a savings account, now is the time to open one. An independent financial advisor will tell you that your emergency cash fund should have between three and 12 months of your current salary saved in it, in case of – as it says on the tin – emergencies. However, if your income protection insurance is comprehensive, three months of living expenses minus your entertainment budget is probably adequate.

It's not a bad idea to consider a less accessible savings account too. The rule of thumb is the harder it is for you to touch, the more interest you will get paid. For example, you might want to move house and need to lay your hands on several thousand pounds in a relative hurry, or the car might be beyond hope and you're reliant on it for work, or taking the kids to school. There's no real limit to the number of savings pots you can have, so get into the habit now.

To give you an idea of my level of organisation (or 'crazy', depending on how you view these things), I have two current accounts and eight savings accounts.

Current Account 1: Monthly direct debits (mortgage, regular bills) spread over each week of the month to smooth out cash flow (if everything comes out on the first of the month and something catastrophic happens in week three and I have emptied the saving accounts, then I have to borrow, which means it's going to cost me more money!).

Current Account 2: Monthly living expenses (food shopping, social, clothes, beer, speeding tickets, alibis, 'I apologise for my behaviour' flowers…)

I also have eight separate savings accounts using different banks for:

- Holidays
- House
- Car
- Christmas
- Son no 1
- Son no 2
- Buffer
- Emergency

I also have a stocks and shares ISA which I max out (this is my priority, but may not be yours) when I can, and a pension.

Each account gets a little bit every month, and I don't carry the cards or details with me so I don't get tempted, or make any drunken eBay purchases. It took a day to set all this up. I only open accounts that have an app, so I can manage them using my phone or PC. Get it sorted and you will feel so much better, even if you are only putting £5 in each one every month.

IMPORTANT NOTE – savings are essential. If you're not already a fan of Money Saving Expert (www.moneysavingexpert.com), acquire the following mindset to make sure your spare cash finds its way to the right place, i.e. your savings accounts:

Do I need it? Can I afford it? Will I use it? Is it worth it?

Wants vs Needs
There is a saying - give a rich person some money, and they will invest it and get it working for them by turning £1 into £2. Give some money to a poor person, and they will buy an iPhone.

Now you know why the rich get richer; they understand compound interest. According to Warren Buffet, compound interest is the eighth wonder of the world. If you don't know who he is, I would highly recommend Googling him and learning!

Basically, if you are going to spend your money, spend it on assets and not on liabilities where you can.

These are fairly easy to lock down. You might think you need a new phone, but do you really just want the latest model? Go to cash-converters or eBay and get a bargain. The same goes for family holidays and days out before you actually leave the military; saving the money for a good holiday to start the new chapter of your life instead is always going to cost you less than a break here and a break there.

My advice here is to go through all of your belongings and sell all of the things you don't use on Facebook (because at the time of writing it's free), or eBay. You'll be surprised how much you can make. I have a clear out every 3 months and what doesn't get sold goes to the charity shop. I would do a car boot, but the thought of getting up at 6am on a Sunday doesn't seem that appealing!

Once you have made a fortune by selling all the crap you don't actually need, we can apply the same mindset to your salary. You might want to earn a six-figure sum, but if you only need to earn half of that, your job prospects will suddenly increase, and with that, the pool of opportunities that will actually give you a life rather than making you a work-slave who never sees their family.

That's not saying you should settle for less. Skills have a variable market rate, and pricing yourself below that market rate is as certain a way not to be hired (or find clients if you intend to set up on your own) as pricing yourself above it. Too low, and potential employers will wonder what's wrong with you; too high, and they'll go for the person who can do the job just as well for several thousand less. That is unless you have read the part of the book on salary negotiation… but more on that later.

Do your research. This means several weeks of scouring job websites and recording salaries and linking them to the area's you think you may want to live in, even if you don't really have much idea of what you want to do yet. That's fine; you'll get some clarity on that as you do your research and as you read this book. If you spot a job and think "I could do that –

and I'd enjoy it", that's one to save to your Job Hunt Spreadsheet that you can also find on www.leavingthemilitary.co.uk.

Credit Cards

Be very wary! I have one, it has a limit of £500 and it's there for emergencies only and doesn't live in my wallet. I am a self-confessed spender and always have been, it makes me happy (I am a child of divorce, so sue me!).

Not a day goes by where I don't find myself looking on eBay and Amazon at stuff I don't need (my accountant Roger can vouch for this). Part of my education in sorting my life out was learning that credit cards are bad debt.

I know how easy it is to accidentally talk yourself into using your credit card by inflating a 'want' into a 'need' in your mind. It's easily done, and the lenders have done a lot of research into making you spend; that's how they make their money. They don't want you to get into trouble where you can't afford to pay, they want to keep you in a happy-medium where you can still live and pay them a bit of interest every month. They are a business and are there to make a profit.

If you do have a lot of credit cards, look at transferring them onto one credit card. There are a lot of comparison credit card websites that can help you. The key is - and you may need to get your Accountability Group involved if you're a spender - to shred your old cards, leave your new card at home and clear the balance while you have a 0% interest window. Do not fall into the trap of keeping hold of the old ones for 'just in case'. You need to go cold turkey, my friend.

Credit Reports

You need to protect your credit report with your life. This is your true passport to how credible you are. I have signed up to the monthly tools offered by the big credit rating agencies, and if I see a change to my file, I am on it like a hawk. I am also a fan of Martin Lewis who has a great website and some great tools for understanding and managing your credit rating.

If you have a poor credit rating, go onto one of the money comparison sites, and there are lots of providers that will happily carry out an eligibility check to see which credit cards would accept your application before you apply. This is great because it doesn't leave a mark on your credit report.

Get a credit card, use it for one thing only like petrol and clear it every month without fail. You will see your credit report improve massively because it shows you are able to act responsibly and lenders will see you improving.

Debt

I left the army £8000 in debt. Literally because I spent all my savings and credit cards on resettlement courses and other courses to get me as prepared as possible. Luckily, I started earning as soon as I left so I could pay this back. However, if your situation is more complicated, then I would encourage you to face this head on and speak to the charity, Step-Change, who are specialists in helping people get out of debt. Do it now: https://www.stepchange.org.

What you need to realise is finance is a big deal in the civilian world. I realised this, which is why I went into project management within financial services – primarily to learn how money works (I'm still learning now!).

In a nutshell, the objective of our economy is to keep money flowing. The faster it moves, the more it makes, and the system is already geared to make it easy for you to spend money you don't yet have. This is done through credit cards, loans and all manner of other financial vehicles. Physical money is disappearing, and electronic and cryptographic money is taking its place, and for the spenders, this is not good. The people in the know are trying to make transactions as frictionless as possible to speed up transactions and make it easier for you to spend money.

For instance, breaking a £20 note is a physical action that is tangible to the senses. I have that small feeling of loss, pockets full of shrapnel afterwards and a sense of regret. However, paying for something via contactless is completely abstract and doesn't have the same feelings attached; who cares? Let's just do it! If you have been to the pub, forgotten your wallet and realised you can pay for a Guinness with your phone or iWatch you will totally get this after the fourth pint!

It's like when you go on holiday and pay for things using a foreign currency. Sometimes you have no idea what you are spending, and it doesn't feel odd or bad because it's abstract. It's only when you get home and realise that you spent £40 on a tube of Hawaiian tropics sun lotion that you realise the cost of the transaction. Yep, this happened to me in Dubai, although I did have a killer tan!

So, don't be embarrassed if you find yourself in debt. The system is geared to get you into to debt. The clever thing is having a plan to get yourself out of it. We all make mistakes and managing your cash is an ongoing battle with the person on the other side of the sales counter who also has a plan to take your cash! So, make sure you have a plan to win.

THIS CHAPTER IN A NUTSHELL

Your Plan of Action
- Get your nearest and dearest to do the 'what do I want to do with my life' exercise. Compare notes and see what you're aligned on. Work together as a team to achieve your goals.
- Go to www.leavingthemilitary.co.uk and download and fill out the following:
  - Logistics Spreadsheet
  - Monthly expenses Spreadsheet
- Review how are bank accounts and savings accounts are structured. Split them up if necessary.
- Get a copy of your credit report and monitor the hell out of it.
- Sort your debt like credit cards out – consolidate where necessary.
- If you have debt, talk to Step-Change (it's confidential).
- Start saving (remember the elephant anatomy?) bite-sized chunks, little and often! – short-term, long-term, and retirement.
- If you need to, liquidise assets (cash in old iPhones, sell things you won't use) to get that three-month buffer.
- Research salaries and jobs.
- Download and start filling out your Job Hunt Spreadsheet.

Things to Note
- The time is always now – however much or little time you have left, start now.
- Well done! Have another pat on the back and another short holiday for getting to the end of Chapter 2.

3 LOOKING AFTER YOURSELF

So here we are.

Even if you're only the hour or so closer to leaving the military that it took you to read the first chapters, you're getting there. It's time to get moving, and this chapter will help you do it. All those dangerous situations you've been in throughout your Forces career? Time to put the clear-thinking and problem-solving skills you've learned into practice.

I will never forget going to an Arnhem reunion and talking to one of the old guys, George, who took part in the D-Day Landings. George told me about a time he and his colleagues were stuck behind enemy lines; no radio, no food or water and very little ammunition left. They stumbled upon a fork in the road, and the group started arguing about which way to go. No one knew they were there, and none of them knew what the future held, or what the consequences of their decisions would be.

George said, "We are taking the left fork." His group didn't agree and continued arguing. George calmed them down and reasoned that he would meet the enemy on his terms, rather than stand there arguing and get taken by surprise.

The moral of the story, and it has stayed with me ever since, is always do something. Never wait for the enemy to come to you, as they will be better prepared than if you go to them.

So, as Blackadder would say, I need a cunning plan!

Remember, forget the noise and concentrate on a solution to the real problem. In this case, the noise was George's colleagues who couldn't decide and were getting themselves more and more worked up. The actual problem was the enemy may very well overrun them via three directions and the longer they did nothing and stood around, the larger the probability of them being taken completely by surprise.

The solution was to be decisive, create a plan and make a decision. George's decision was based on the only factors he could change and not the ones he couldn't. If they were going to meet the enemy, then they would do it on their terms and to their plan. Also cutting down on the directions an ambush could potentially come from by being alert and on the move.

Remember, always do something. Do not fall foul of 'analysis paralysis', it will kill you.

Staying Positive

So here you are at your very own fork in the road. If you're feeling nervous, that's fine. If you're feeling excited, that's also fine. Remember, doing something is far better than doing nothing and getting overrun.

Make the situation work for you, and use that nervous energy to get yourself ready. Remember the positive mental attitude section at the end of chapter one? Well, this next part will help you bolster that positive mental attitude and get you in a good place to be decisive.

As you know, I am an avid learner, and when I took my first business to Cranfield Management School, I was introduced to the Golden Circles. Now you probably haven't heard of Simon Sinek, a leadership expert famous for the concept of 'Find Your Why'. Have a look on YouTube for him. It's the best 30 minutes you will invest (after reading my book of course).

We have touched on it briefly already in Chapter One, but knowing your 'why', your purpose, is going to be your best friend over the coming weeks and months. It will be the difference between finding a job and carving out a career. There's nothing wrong with the former, but if you're picking up a book to help with your transition out of the military and into civilian life, you're probably after the latter.

Think back to your basic training. Part of that was learning your place in the command chain and how the chain worked. Civilian life doesn't quite work like that. In the military, you knew where you were, where you were headed, and how to get there. Your path – with aptitude tests and promotion courses thrown in to determine what you were good at – was set. It was kind of clear, and I think you will agree when you have been out of the services a few years, very comforting.

Civilian life is considerably less linear. A management path is potentially full of sidesteps and even backward steps, and it's down to you, not your boss. There's no set path, and no single way to skin that particular rabbit. Not to mention you can get fired (not impossible, but nevertheless much, much harder in the military!), possibly made redundant (apparently, this will happen on average three times in your working life), reshuffled, reorganised, and just plain shunted into a job that wasn't the one you applied to do and were hired for.

On top of this, there are the changes you make when you decide to go and work for someone else. It can be hard to see where you may end up if you don't know what you're aiming for. If your 'why' isn't clear, you could just be evading the noise, rather than solving the problem.

In many ways, we military people have been cosseted to an extent – I'm not saying for one minute that the military is an easy option, it isn't. But we have had most of the underlying infrastructure laid out for us: food, medical, dentist, post etc., and our career paths were fairly transparent and easy to understand.

I know it probably didn't feel like it, and I can only talk about my experiences of making it to the dizzy heights of a Corporal Gazelle Pilot. But in comparison to what I did, and then the trials and tribulations I faced when becoming a civilian, I certainly felt well looked after in the military. Not saying I pray for an urn of range tea or a bag of bacon and beans rations from 1978 for dinner, but you get the point I'm trying to make.

TLA's (Three Letter Acronyms)

When it comes to staying positive, another idiosyncrasy I had to overcome was military jargon. After 14 years I was well and truly immersed in military language and talking to civilians was just bizarre. We both spoke English, but the subtle nuances of meaning made it hard for me to connect when I first left. I had to open my mind to the possibility that I needed to change my language. My days of answering, "Tea Standard NATO please," when asked if I wanted a drink have now changed to, "Tea, white two sugars please."

Informing your new work colleagues that you are off for a 'shovel recce', followed by a 'wet' will probably get you sectioned. Best to use plain English.

I mention all of this because you need to be able to articulate your 'Why' in language that a three-year-old can understand. You need to test it constantly. What you say and what people hear are often two separate things, so test and adjust.

You may very well feel that nobody understands you. Indeed, my sense of humour has got me into hot water on more than one occasion, and my language (while utterly hilarious) completely missed the target with my new civilian counterparts. I might as well have been speaking Martian. Be clear, keep it to plain English and test and adjust your language. Communication is so important, and it is so easy to get wrong. So remember KISS (keep it simple stupid). Otherwise, you can feel very isolated, and that leads to the next bit…

Think Negative Thoughts

Not literally, obviously. But it's a good idea to get out of an "it'll all be okay" mindset, because it won't unless you make it okay. Time spent planning is never wasted, so use your resettlement time, in fact, all of your time, wisely. There are plenty of resources and a discussion group on www.leavingthemilitary.co.uk that can help if you're struggling.

Think back to the last time you had to do something urgently, and there was no getting out of it. These times are usually moments of crisis in our lives, and we tend to focus on them in total aggression-mode in order to power through, get things done, and get past it.

This is the moment when determination and courage kick in, and you just face forward and go. Great. That's what you need now, but you need to find a way to channel that without it being disaster-management-mode. For that, you need to discipline yourself to find your 'why'. And that's something familiar to you already.

If you're in a place that's quite dark, I have a brilliant little technique that gets me through. It's called Task Bingo.

It starts with three lists. This is how I run my life. I know what you're thinking…freak show… me having more than 1 list - what are the odds.

My Three Lists for Managing My Life

Can Do List

This is a list of every job I need to do between now and eternity. All the things that matter to me.

To Do List

These are prioritised tasks from my Can Do List. These are tasks or parts of tasks that I need to do this week/month/period of time.

Must Do List

Again, these are tasks that are prioritised from my To Do List that need to be done or started TODAY. I also put any unexpected tasks that come flying in from stage right. That way I can make a decision on what I'm not going to do and manage any expectations I need to (e.g. tell someone I'm going to be late).

This is all sounding a bit… hmmm, uncomfortable…

Sadly, I'm human. I wake up some mornings, and no matter how much I want to, I just cannot be bothered. Damn the consequences, I want to run the other way for a day and watch Top Gear on Dave when it was good (I haven't seen the new one on Amazon yet, so don't judge me too harshly). In short, we all have these days.

So, I break out Task Bingo.

I look at my Must Do List and prioritise it again and take the top 80% of the tasks and put them into squares like a bingo card. I put all the hard tasks first in a line. Always tackle the horrible tasks first thing in the morning, that way you can enjoy the rest of the day with a vague sense of accomplishment.

If I have managed to tick off a line, I try and go for the whole card. Which is normally 80% of my Must Do List, which is what I originally wanted to achieve that day. I turn it into a game and give myself a break. It's ok to give yourself a break. Even uber-humble and modest Adonis ex-Army Air Corps sky gods like me have bad days.

So how do I keep it together? I use an app on my phone called Wunderlist for this. I share the lists with, you guessed it… My Accountability Group and they berate and chastise me accordingly when I'm not pulling my weight.

So what does my task list consist of? Well, normally it's whatever bit of the elephant I am trying to eat.

If it's getting a job, I start at the end with what sort of job best fits my latest version of 'what do I want to do with my life'. Remember, I do this at least every six months, and I suggest you do this too. If it's writing a book, it's about what will give me the most enjoyment and transfer the most value to my readers. Believe it or not, every chapter in this book is in my Wunderlist iPhone app!

What should go on your list? Anything you want to get done. No matter where you are in the process. This is a technique to keep you delivering the goods. Share it with your Accountability Group to ensure you follow through and keep your promises.

Motivation and Keeping Going

So, now you have some lists and some tools on how to get your plan together using what you want to do with your life, and you have a spreadsheet for your finances and some lists and prioritisation tools to execute your tasks.

An important point to make here is that my lists are there to be exploited by you to help you get the life that aligns with you, and these should all revolve around your 'why'. If you're still unsure where to go next, there's more on making lists on www.leavingthemilitary.co.uk, and I will also deal with this in more detail in later books.

But how do you keep motivated? Let me share my tips for all the people who are not massive fans of my positive mental attitude stuff. Hopefully this is another way of describing the same principle a different way.

Motivation starts with action. Action drives and feeds motivation.

People think it's the other way around, but in my experience, it doesn't work like that. Let me give you an example. Now, I like to stay fit, but there was a time in my life where I piled on the pounds and managed to 'occupy too much space'. By that, I mean I should have been on a documentary. The minute an old colleague (ok, I'll fess up, it was my five-year-old son) asked why his mates were saying that his dad was a bit of a 'wok smuggler', I knew that I needed to do something. Five-year-olds don't normally lie to save your feelings – mine don't. So I knew I had to do something and wearing stripy stuff that apparently makes you look thin just wasn't cutting it...

How did I do it? Simple. I put my gym kit on and then decided if I wanted to go to the gym, or for a run, not the other way around. My mind was telling me it was going to hurt and I couldn't be bothered. But on the other hand, I was already dressed, so maybe just run to the end of the road. Before you knew it, I was out the door having a very slow jog. Would that have happened if I had decided first and then put my sports kit on? Err No. I would probably be blogging about sausage rolls and not writing this book.

Action first and then the motivation will come. Once it's there, the perspiration and achievement will follow. Nobody motivates themselves out of bed in the morning, the action gets them out of bed. Your actions should have brought you this far, now it's time to keep that fire burning and get you really motivated. Feeling that positive mental attitude kicking in yet? If not, take a short holiday and go back and read the previous chapters.

So what else helps? Think of someone that really inspires you. Not just someone you respect, but someone that makes you want to go that extra mile, someone you would buy a Ginsters, or even drag yourself around one more circuit for. That's what you're aiming for. Sit down with your notebook, and write down what the qualities you admire are.

Try using the 'what do I want to do with my life' exercise on them to help you. Try to imagine the answers they would come up with. Why do they make you drag your backside through things you'd rather avoid? What's their special sauce? What do you need to concentrate on in yourself to have the same effect on others around you? Wouldn't it be great if you could get them in your Accountability Group? Just a thought!

Even if you don't know them, but their words resonate with you, print them out and get them on the fridge, on your bathroom mirror, anywhere where you can read them once a day. God damn it, go get it tattooed on something that you look at every day (not your mother in law. They don't like it. I know. But that's a story for my other books...).

Another good tip here is having your end outcome in mind from the start. Something visible that is easy to understand. But how do you do that? Remember JFK? If you don't, put down the G&T and go back to the previous chapter - you're hilarious! (If you see someone else reading this book, and they are frantically flicking through the pages, my bet is they're drunk on G&Ts).

So, with that in mind, what is your 'man on the moon statement'? Maybe it's time to have a chat with your Accountability Group. They may send you to AA, they may wrap a cold, wet towel around your heads to get you thinking. Either way, the future is bright my friend, keep going.

Action Steps
1. Start at the End
   - In 20 years' time, what does success mean to you? Can you define your 'man on the moon' statement?
   - Does it align to your why?
   - Can you say it in a sentence to a complete stranger and they get it?
2. Now, Start at the Beginning
   - Look at the results of your 'what do I want to do with my life' exercise.
   - How does this translate to problems that you could fix for others that appeal to you?
   - Can your Accountability Group help you translate this into a job?
   - Does it sound appealing and something that gives you that feeling of purpose?
3. Acid-test question: If you were doing this for the rest of your life, would you feel excited by it?

If the answer is yes, can you make enough money from it? If not, it doesn't mean it's a lost cause, you just need to do some research on how you could monetise it. There are a lot of chat forums available on the internet that can help. Failing that, post a question on the discussion group on www.leavingthemilitary.co.uk and someone will be able to help you.

4. How does it align to your 'man on the moon' statement?
Now, this is fairly hairy stuff and quite overwhelming when you think about it. The key here is to take bite-sized chunks to eat your elephant. You're looking long-term, and as I said above, looking at where you'll be in 20 years' time, so you may want to do the above every 6 months to ensure you are on track.

I do, but let's face it, I'm a bit crazy, which is fine. But you bought my book. Hilarious!

All joking aside, people are always subconsciously overwhelmed with time. They overestimate what they can do in a year, but completely underestimate what they can achieve in a decade. Look at how one sentence from JFK inspired a nation to achieve the impossible in less than nine years. Remember, one bite at a time.

People don't buy WHAT you do; they buy WHY you do it.

Say what? This is a true statement when we're talking at the 'planning the rest of my life' level.

It's not good enough to be skilled enough at something that someone will pay you to do it. You need to understand the magic trio – why, what, and how. Remember, the 'why' needs to be simple enough for you to understand and explain it in one sentence (think about George and the Arnhem Landings!). Then we need to make it transparent enough that complete strangers get it in under five seconds. The what and the how should then be fairly easy to explain.

So, for example, you might be good at washing the car (and someone else will happily pay you to do that), but can you imagine doing it for the rest of your working life? Well, only if it fulfils your 'why' first, and excites you every day.

You might love helping others, and be really good at sorting their lives out for them – will people pay you to do that? Sure. You've just described being a Life Coach. This book isn't to turn out a generation of life coaches, of course, but to underline again and again the necessity of finding something long-term and sustainable that people will pay you to do. And that you love.

How Do You Find Your Why?
Your support network can help here. And that's not just your immediate family and the friends you have now, it's also the people you knew when you were growing up, were at school/college/university with, served with (and who have already left the military). It's also extended family, cousins that you used to knock around with, and in short, anyone who has a stable, civilian life that you can lean on for support. Social and business network lines are as blurred in civilian life as they are in the military, so don't turn down that boring barbeque if it's a potential opportunity to network.

It can help to think of your why in terms of purpose:
- What do you want long-term? (These are your life aspirations rather than your business aspirations).
- What impact do you want to have with what you do, and how you will define success?
- How you are going to put this into action? (In your case, this is how you're going to track down that job – or even make your own).

It can also help you get those work priorities in order:

- Who you want to work for
- Where you need to live to work there
- When you need to start work
- What can you see yourself doing?
- Why do you want to do it?

And a final 'W':

WOAH! – it can be useful to put the handbrake on from time to time to make sure you have the right skills and qualifications for where you're aiming, and to revisit your priorities and goals to see if there's anything else you need to be doing.

Your 'why' might take a while, but if you get that right, you'll discover a new single-mindedness of purpose which will make that job hunt much easier; not necessarily quicker, but easier. And that's because you'll come across as passionate, engaged, and on-message.

But back to finding the why. To be clear, your 'why' is not benefit or profit. Of course, you need to earn enough to live, but if times are tough, you need more than money to keep you getting up in the morning. "Because I want to make money" isn't a solid reason, money is a mere consequence. "Because I want to use my business skills to help my company (or my family) be the best at what they do and to benefit people" is a solid reason.

Money brings opportunity, not happiness. The positive application of knowledge brings happiness.

Back to the Self-Care Bit...

Human beings need to do more than just survive; they need to live. That means enjoying life and seeking professional help if you need it. That's not weak, that's strong. If it's not your choice to leave, particularly if you've experienced life-changing circumstances that are taking you out of the military for good, you might be propping yourself up in ways that aren't entirely sensible right now, either for you or for your family.

If you need help with drug or alcohol issues, seek it now. Even if you're only an occasional problem user.

For alcohol problems – www.alcoholics-anonymous.org.uk
For general help, particularly for your family – www.adfam.org.uk
For mental health advice in general – www.mind.org.uk

I'll say it again: Seeking help is a sign of strength. Staying quiet is a sign of weakness.

It takes a strong person to identify and admit that things need to change going forward and to find the necessary support network to deal with that. It can be very easy to lose sight of what you're getting up for, especially if you feel that you're failing not just yourself but your family. We don't just need to survive, we need to live. And just being a salary slave won't get you there.

Finding your personal 'why' is going to help you live, give you the motivation and conviction to take the right kind of risks, and help you stay on track. It is not the easiest of tasks, but you will get far more benefit out of understanding your 'why' in comparison to the effort you put in.

THIS CHAPTER IN A NUTSHELL

Your Plan of Action
- Stay positive – this doesn't mean sticking your head up your backside and saying, "everything's fine."
- Work out the intersection between what you love doing, what you're good at, and then translate that into what people will pay you to do – there's your job.
- Find and always keep refining your 'why'.
- Can Do, To Do, Must Do. Prioritise your plan into bite-sized chunks.
- Task Bingo - have it on hand for the duvet days!
- If you have found your 'why', but you're not sure how to monetise it, get onto some forums, or post a question on www.leavingthemilitary.co.uk.
- If you're relying on the bottle or taking drugs, get help now - some companies even carry out random drug tests on employees.
- Give yourself a break and don't be too hard on yourself if this isn't coming naturally. Get people around you to help you clarify your thoughts.

Things to Note
- Money is nice, but it shouldn't be your motivator – being a salary slave won't help you when times are tough. Knowledge will.
- There's more to building happiness and a career than finding a job.
- Asking for help is a sign of strength, staying quiet is a sign of weakness.
- Money brings opportunity, not happiness. The positive application of knowledge brings happiness.

4 GETTING YOURSELF JOB READY

Interestingly, I was fired from my first job out of the military. It was a large car sales firm that had numerous branches, and I was their IT Manager. I did a software audit, and I found that for the 1000 PCs, I could only find one serial number for their day to day software.

I went to see the CEO to explain that I needed a large sum of money to make the company compliant and was told that he didn't have this on his own computer, and he would be damned if he was paying for it at work.

Understandably, I went on to explain that as a business, we were making money using software that we hadn't paid for, and tried to explain the risks as best and as transparently as I could. Obviously, I pushed too hard as the next day I was dragged in to be told by HR that I wasn't really a team player and was sacked for gross negligence.

The moral of the story is that I wasn't reading the situation at all, and I was oblivious to the vast difference between their values and subsequent culture and my own. I was trying to negotiate with a car salesman and was trying to do the right thing when he only wanted to pay for the licences at the very last moment.

It taught me one important lesson: Only apply to companies whose values are easy to evidence, and you can see the values at work. This creates the company's culture. And I don't mean posters on the wall. Look on www.glassdoor.co.uk. It's a bit like trip advisor for companies where employees can leave anonymous feedback. You need to take some of the reviews with a pinch of salt, but it can arm you with some very surgical questions to ask if you get an interview.

I digress, let's get back on point. Looking back, getting fired was awful at the time, but it was the best thing that could have happened to me. It woke me up to what drives businesses. Plus, I went on to earn more money because of my new-found understanding.

Getting yourself ready for work in the civilian world isn't as simple as buying a suit and finding a job. You will need to change your whole mindset. If you don't, you won't last long in any job you find, or in any self-employed enterprise you undertake.

This won't be because you're bad at it, but as we've said before, civilian life is nothing like the military. You will be used to working exceptionally hard, and perhaps even working non-stop until the job is done. But unless you learn how to pace yourself you'll be looking at serious burnout very fast – and that will take you out of the workplace for some time.

This chapter will make you feel like you're back at school, but in many ways, you are. I'm not going to sugar coat how tough it is out there; even for someone who has all the qualifications and many years of experience on top. Why should an employer look at you, ex-military with little or no civilian workplace experience, and probably fewer (academic) letters after your name?

Funnily enough, and here is a top tip for all of you Regimental Sergeant Majors out there. RSM generally means Regional Sales Manager out here, and interestingly I have seen a few RSM's treated with a lot less deference and respect than they are used to after they have proudly announced that they were an RSM to an unwitting civilian.

There are many good reasons why an employer should and will employ you. What we need to do is take your skills and translate them into something a hiring manager is looking for. But you're going to have to work hard to get there, so make sure you use your Accountability Group to help identify skills that you might not think are such a big deal, but that an employer would consider gold dust.

Your CV Only Gets You the Interview, You Get the Job

A CV is a sales brochure. It has to sell you at the salary you are looking for, and its job is to get you an interview. It has to create enough intrigue so that a hiring manager would want to meet you. Got it?

Now, every time I applied for a role, I tailored my CV, and this is so important. What I used to do is print the job advert/description out and get three different colour highlighter pens. I would highlight every skill in one colour, keywords in another colour and personality and strengths in another colour.

I would then ensure that every piece of text that I had highlighted was in my two-page CV. I would also make sure that most of the highlighted points were in the first half of the first page.

Why? Because that is normally the only bit hiring managers read on their first pass. Imagine if you had a hundred CVs to go through, how much would you read? A good rule of thumb here is that if your CV chimes with the job advert in the first half page, you'll probably get an interview. It's just elementary my dear Watson!

So, your CV is the most important piece of paper you'll have in terms of bagging that killer job, and successfully ensuring that you spend the rest of your working days living your 'why' to its full earning potential.

Yes, it's even more important than your exam certificates or any other professional qualifications. It's a document of you, and it should give a – professional – essence of you before you get as far as the interview room.

If you're not great with words, you might be tempted to get someone to write it for you, but this would be a huge, catastrophic, monumental, and potentially damaging mistake. Beyond getting some of your most meticulous and pedantic friends to check your grammar and spelling for you, it should be written by you and reflect who you are, and should 'sound' like you on the page.

Professional CV writing services have grown in the last couple of years, and many are preying on people who think they will never find another job. And to be honest, they're often not worth the money you're spending on them. It's an unregulated industry, and the people doing it are low paid and only have experience of getting themselves a job as a CV writer.

Prior to writing this book, I tested this out. I paid a top London firm £1500 to rewrite my CV and was less than impressed. So there, I have just saved you £1500!

However, I spent £50 on www.peopleperhour.com to get someone to edit, format and proofread it and it came back with all my content, but looking great. £50 well spent!

A sobering thought for you is that if a CV writer produces your CV, you can lay awake at night knowing that all the other CVs that your CV writer has written will look and sound just like yours.

Excellent! Your CV will not stand out, it will be full of big impressive words that are completely intangible and will not sell your 'why'. By all means, go and have a chat with a recruitment professional about how best to present yourself to a particular client, but no one's going to write the story of you like you can.

When I first left the Army, I went to see a company who promised me access to the 'secret job market' and would work with me and make my CV worth £100k. All they wanted was £8000 up front. Do not do it. I repeat, DO NOT GIVE THEM YOUR MONEY!! Companies like this make a fortune off of vulnerable people who don't have a plan and are fearful for the future. Their sales patter is well-honed, and it's understandable why people fall for this sort of stuff, but you need to learn to write your own CV.

I spent my last year asking everybody and anyone 'what do you not like about my CV?' and I mean everyone! From HR Managers to admin staff, to accountants, to teachers and of course everyone in my Accountability Group. Their job or role wasn't important, I just wanted their opinion.

I made sure to ask what they didn't like, just to get objective feedback. This is an important tactic because a lot of your friends will just tell you your CV is awesome to hurt your feelings. Ask them to be brutally honest. For me, it really helped me to understand what I thought I had written and what people had actually read and understood from it.

The Magic Rule of CVs: MAKE IT TANGIBLE

Think about it, if I told you there were loads of the enemy about to overrun us, the answer you would want to know is, is it 10, or 10,000, what direction are they coming from, what weapons do they have etc.?

The person reading your CV has to get a tangible feel for what you were responsible for regarding time, manpower, money, who you reported to, what you achieved, what was at stake etc. Make it tangible! Get your Accountability Group to read it. If they say, 'So what?' it isn't tangible enough yet.

Get your reviewers to ask you 'why' five times regarding every point on your CV. This will help you boil your points down to the problems that you solved and what the achievements were in relation to the benefits.

What Your CV Needs to Include

1. Your full name. Obviously.
2. The area you live in. I never put my full address on my CV because I don't want to publish to all and sundry where I live. You never know who might see your CV and where your personal details may end up. This is your call though.
3. A mobile number with a professional answerphone message (not the jokey, rude one you recorded with your mates on the last tour you did). If you need to get a dual SIM phone, get one, and make sure you use the right number.
4. A professional email address. If you have to create a new one for your job-hunting exploits, do so. You might even want to consider buying an appropriate domain name, so that your email address can only belong to you, and is memorable for potential employers (i.e. mail@johnsmith.com). This doesn't cost a lot, and it's a worthwhile investment, especially if you plan on setting up on your own at some point in the future.

I have seen CVs with some hilarious email addresses on. I am not a gambling man, but I am pretty sure that chris.hitchens@studly.co.uk will not increase my gravitas and credibility (which is a real shame, as I have just checked, and the domain is available).

5. A short summary of who you are and what you do. Remember, the person reading it is going to be thinking, "What's in it for me, why should I see this person?" Talk tangibly and relate things to time, cost and quality.
6. An opening statement. The opening statement on your CV (often called a professional overview) is a great way to give your prospective employer a real feel for who you are and what you do, and most importantly, your 'why'. Also, should you choose to – explain why you're leaving the Forces, and what positive qualities it has given you.
7. Your employment history with your most recent job/responsibilities (i.e. the military), at the top. If that's all you've got to put there, that's fine. Some people stay in the same job for the same length of time – start to think of it in the same way.

Do not write pages and pages of waffle. Keep it short and sharp and absolutely no longer than 3 pages. Two pages is better, three pages is acceptable. Any more than that and it becomes soft, strong and very absorbent. No one wants to read a 16-page CV, no matter how interesting you think you are.

Concentrate on what you were responsible for, what you achieved, what level you reported at, the budget you looked after, number of people you coordinated or looked after and the quality standards you needed to achieve. Always think in Time, Cost and Quality when writing your CV. This is a great way to ensure it's tangible and that the reader can relate to your skills and achievements.

8. Other relevant information. This can include qualifications, although don't worry about listing every subject, or even necessarily every grade. For example, if you have a degree, listing the number of A Levels and GCSEs you have will be adequate. State any foreign languages you speak, and the level of fluency, and also whether you hold a driving licence.

You don't need to put your age or your hobbies, these are only worth mentioning if they demonstrate a skill the employer would benefit from.

The Golden Rule: If your CV has information that does not offer value to the job you are applying for, take it off. It's wasting valuable space.

If you're really struggling, I have posted a CV template, and a good version of a CV on www.leavingthemilitary.co.uk. Feel free to pinch and plagiarise to get you going.

Things to Note

I have already mentioned that Military life is full of jargon. So is civilian life – jargon that's really unfamiliar to you anyway. But those letters that make perfect sense to you in your CV will mean zilch to a potential employer.

Don't assume that Forces job titles will make sense to the outside world either; practice explaining exactly what it is that you do and what it involves. Practice it in the mirror if you have to. Remember, RSM in the military means Regimental Sergeant Major. In civilian life, it means Regional Sales Manager!

Helpful hint: Use the job title (Google is any employer's friend, so don't worry about trying to 'civilianify' job titles), but then use bullet points to list your duties, such as overseeing staff, responsibility for budgets. Remember - Time, Cost and Quality.

The Special Hell that is the Covering Letter

No one likes these. Anyone who tells you they do is lying, and they don't have any friends. They are the equivalent of being interrogated while naked. That said, I am sympathetic to the fact that some of the Royal Marines I know really enjoy this sort of caper!

Even if you're confident about your skills, qualifications, and abilities, there's a good chance you'll find yourself almost apologising for them in your covering letter. Is there any way around this? The good news is yes, there is.

Instead of apologising or justifying, give an example of when you used this skill. Another good use of your covering letter is to demonstrate your knowledge about the company. For example, they might have recently hit the news for an innovative product, or for a charitable donation. State that this makes them a company you'd like to work for and why. Remember the 'why' bit from earlier on? A covering letter is a great place to explain your 'why'.

Helpful hint: Best not to mention any negative news, should there be any.

A lot of applications don't require these anymore, but if you find yourself in need, go to sites like www.peopleperhour.co.uk, Freelancer, or Fiverr and you'll find people who have some really well-written templates that you can craft into your own literary masterpiece for £10. They will also proofread your CV for you as well, very helpful!

The Tough Bit

Just to set your expectations from the start, the job market is currently extremely difficult. Especially – at the time of writing – as the UK's position with regard to some ongoing working relationships, not just with Europe, but with the rest of the world, are very unclear. This is likely to affect not just the job market but how we work for decades to come, so it's hardly putting an expiry date on this chapter by putting that out there.

It's entirely likely that you'll experience something like a 1 in 60 response rate for cold approaches, and the vast majority of those will be "no thanks". That's not to say that cold approaches are a waste of your time. Think of your CV as being like a fur coat on sale in summer – it isn't needed then, but HR could very well file it away for when the cold weather hits and it will be ideal. A 'no' now, or even no response now, doesn't mean it will be no forever.

What You Can Do Now

Stay positive and keep working on you; particularly 'you the brand' (more on this in Chapter Six).

Remember, everybody gets rejected. Steve Jobs was fired from his own company and bounced back. Rejection is just part of the journey, learn to use it as a learning exercise and find out what you can improve on.

Fill any gaps in your qualifications that might make you 'second choice' on paper before you even get to interview; at the very least, this means making sure you have a clear pass for English and Maths at GCSE level.

Above all, be nice, no matter how frustrating. Yes, you might want to fire a verbal barrage that would be worthy of a scene from that film 'A few good Men', but trust me, 'they can't handle the truth'. It's just that you're one of many candidates, so be nice. You catch more bees with honey...

You might want to approach a recruiter (more on this in the next chapter) to help you with your job search. If you're trying to break into a company where recruitment tends to be an inside job, you're going to need all the assistance you can get.

Telling people things like, 'You, Haircut Monday', 'Next time plug the iron in champ, it helps' or 'Oi you, Gandalf! Stand closer to your razor next time', whilst hilarious will make people think that you're related to Windsor Davies from It Ain't Half Hot Mum.

Personally, I think you're hilarious and would love to have a pint with you, but would I employ you? Probably not. You'd scare the locals.

The Interview
The 7P's: Proper Planning and Preparation Prevents Piss-Poor Performance.

I am sure that you will have heard that one a few times, but it rings true here too. Some things to do with your preparation are obvious; turn up clean and well-presented, (which means fully dressed if you're from the Navy/Royal Marines) and on time (which means five minutes early if you're from the RAF).

However, it also means researching the company, and second-guessing a few questions you might get asked. These might include:

• Tell us about your key strengths

- What is your major weakness? (always turn these into a positive!)
- Where do you see yourself five years from now?
- Why do you want to work here?
- What kind of salary are you looking for in this role?
- (And worst of all…) Do you have any questions?

They're all, in their way, trick questions, as our natural instinct is to make excuses for ourselves or to give a response that is too over-confident and off-putting to a potential employer.

Q&A Time...

Here are a few helpful ideas to make them work for you:

Question: Give us a few of your strengths

Answer: The job advert/description will tell you what strengths they are looking for. Remember my little highlighter ritual? Get a highlighter, highlight the key phases and think about how your strength and skills align to these phrases. Another good tip is to read their website, it should have their company 'core values' on. These are practically the answer to this question.

For instance, use your service record to demonstrate loyalty as one of your great strengths. Also, use the fact that the camaraderie you've experienced with your colleagues shows that you're a team player and your attitude to seeing a task through to completion. Completer-Finishers are worth their weight in gold.

When your boss told you to stand to attention and get your heels together, this actually translates to one of your key strengths. This was more than you demonstrating drill moves that would make a guardsman blush. This my friend actually means that you are able to really listen to your client's needs and then execute them to the highest standards and demonstrate the benefits.

Question: What is your major weakness?

Answer: For ex-Forces, this is an easy one. You're honest and tenacious, and sometimes have to be told when to take a break, or even sometimes to admit defeat when there is no further value to be had, but the little completer-finisher in you wants to keep going. Anyone employing you knows that you'll go the extra mile. But to be fair, whenever I was asked this question, the answer was always "chocolate".

Question: Where do you see yourself five years from now?

Answer: This is a tricky one; aiming for a position too high within the company might be seen as arrogant, whereas aiming low might be seen as lacking in ambition. A good answer to this one is to say something along the lines of learning and utilising the knowledge to make a valuable difference within the team, and hopefully, be given a chance to demonstrate your leadership qualities by making the most of the opportunities presented to you. Again, think about time, cost and quality.

Question: Why do you want to work here?
Answer: This is where your company research will pay dividends. You want to work there because your research has highlighted that this company aligns to your purpose, your 'why'. A good question for you is if they don't align to your 'why', then why do you want to work there?

Question: What kind of salary are you looking for in this role?
Answer: This is such a loaded question, but it's likely to come up. The best way to deal with it is to bat the question right back and ask what kind of salary they're planning to offer.

The first person to mention a figure almost always loses the negotiation – it's a scientific fact. If they send the question straight back to you, use the bracketing technique (i.e. between £30k and £39k), rather than a solid number. And then be quiet.

Silence is your friend in a negotiation. Let the silence linger. In all my years, this technique has earned me more than I ever thought possible.

When an employer has said a figure, let's say £20,000 for ease of maths. I always used to look a bit rejected and look at my shoes and shut up. Five to ten seconds later a higher figure would come and then I would use science to my advantage.

They have mentioned the figure, so I would double the figure. If they have added an extra £1000 to the salary making it £21,000, I would respond by adding another £1000 taking the salary to £22,000, knowing full well we would negotiate and probably end up around £21,500. That is an extra £1500 for saying nothing.

Just please don't go and spend this on having your CV written by a top London firm.

I said at the beginning of the book that I plan to write more books focused on CVs, interviews and the dreaded salary negotiation, so keep an eye out for those and if you have any questions or points in the meantime, you can ask them on www.leavingthemilitary.co.uk.

Needless to say, though, make sure your lifestyle figure is at the very bottom of your bracket (remember your budget plan?). There are several sites of varying degrees of reliability which will give you rough ballpark figures for salaries for positions similar to the one you're being interviewed for.

Question: Do you have any questions?

Answer: You probably have all kinds of questions that aren't quite appropriate to ask, but if you ask nothing else, ask this, "What have you enjoyed most about working for the firm?"

An engaged, enthusiastic employee won't hesitate with all kinds of anecdotes and successes. If they're hard pushed to find anything, you might want to think twice about whether you and that company are a good fit after all. My favourite question is, "What do you not like about working here, or what would you change?" This shows that you are serious and want to know the truth.

Also, remember www.glassdoor.co.uk? This can give you some great questions where you can really probe their values and how these translate into their culture. Ask away! If questions like this rattle the interviewers then you have all you need to know, and you've had a lucky escape. You may not get the job, but at least you know that their values only go as far as the posters on the wall and the company doesn't live and breathe them.

As I have mentioned earlier in the book, the job description/advert for a job is normally out of date after your first day on the job. No plan ever survives the first bullet and all that. I always say to the interviewers, "If I was successful in securing the job, and I was to start next Monday, could you walk me through exactly what the day would look like, what would I be doing, how could I add value from day one?"

Now, this is a great technique. Psychologically, it makes the interviewer subconsciously think about offering you the job, then they have to sell the job to you, and even if they don't like you, they will still work hard to sell the role to you. This is your opportunity to point out any skills you might have missed and a final chance to clarify why you would be the obvious choice.

One more note on interview questions; presumably, if you're targeting a particular company or job sector, you have some kind of emotional pull towards it. Work on that, and prepare answers that stem from your passion for the job, and your skills as a problem-solver. Fit the skills you highlighted in the job advert into your answers and you will be talking in their language.

How you look for a job often demonstrates how you will act in a job once you have it.

After the interview, I always used to post a letter on nice paper, with a nice handwritten envelope via special delivery to each interviewer thanking them for their time and how much I am looking forward to working with them. Everyone likes to feel important and valued, and everyone likes receiving a letter that isn't a bill or a court summons. This can increase your chances, so investing in the postage can make you stand out.

Should I Take Any Job?

That's a good question. If you don't have much in terms of cash reserves, then yes, you might be in a position where you have to take the first job that's offered to you. Just remember what you're stepping into if their values don't match your own. Keep your opinions to yourself, work hard to get a good reference and keep looking for your next job.

However, if you don't want to be forced into that position, then consider temping through an agency, especially if it's in a position that will offer you new skills, such as learning specific software packages that you might not be familiar with.

Look for contracts that run for 6 to 12 weeks and keep looking for that next job at all times. At worst, it's going to give you an insight into what civilian working life is like (and just how alien it can seem), and at best, you'll be better prepared for going into the right job. Additionally, £12 an hour for taking the post round is a lot better than £0 an hour for watching daytime television.

If you need money – and especially if you have debt – don't be proud. Your creditors are obliged to take your personal circumstances into account, but they won't take kindly to you not earning anything when it comes to working out a repayment schedule. Sometimes these jobs are merely temporary stepping stones to paying the bills while you're in search of your 'why'.

These sorts of jobs are temporary and do not define you. One of the jobs I did whilst waiting for a secure proper job, was as an unsalaried, commission-only kitchen salesman. It was a horrendous pressure sales door to door job and not something I was particularly proud of doing.

In fact, it was so far away from my 'why' I felt dirty afterwards. Not that there's anything wrong with kitchen salespeople, the guy who did our kitchen was lovely! But the way this company went about it was cut-throat, and that's me being polite.

But looking back, it showed me exactly what my 'why' wasn't and helped me understand sales, the mindset and the dirty techniques immensely.

If you are interested in buying a rare one of a kind beech shaker-style kitchen with free appliances, then please go to my website and put down a 90% deposit. I'm joking (we only have it in oak...).

THIS CHAPTER IN A NUTSHELL

Your Plan of Action
- Go on www.glassdoor.co.uk to learn about a company's values and culture.
- Use some of the reviews to help you write interview questions that you what to ask them.
- Learn how to read job adverts and highlight all the keywords and skills.
- Write your CV.
- Tailor your CV for every application.
- Use the CV Template on www.leavingthemilitary.co.uk.
- If you see something worded well in a CV that explains what you did better than how you could say it, then plagiarise!
- Find answers that work for you for common interview questions using the job advert and their website.
- Fill the gaps in your skills (I'll say it again, it's really tough out there).
- Prepare your questions for the interview. Probe how their values translate into their culture.
- Drive to the interview location a day before and do a recce if needed, so you're not late on the day.
- Practice salary negotiation with your Accountability Group.
- Take a job (any job) to gain 'civilian workplace' skills (plus, Bargain Hunt's not that great these days).

Things to Note
- I'll say it again – it's tough out there. You might not get the job overnight. But you've made a career out of being persistent once, and you will again.
- Get yourself job ready, and do it now.

5 JOBS AND RECRUITERS

We briefly covered getting yourself and your CV ready for interviews. But what about the recruitment industry, LinkedIn, and networking?

Before you deal with this chapter, sit down with a trusted member of your Accountability Group. You'll have ideas about what kind of salary you need to earn and where you want to live, but you might still be unclear on what sort of job you actually want; permanent, contract, part-time, agency etc. That's where you need to do some more work.

Going it Alone, or Using a Recruitment Company?

If you're lucky enough to be in a position to take your time looking for your next career – perhaps you've built up a significant financial buffer, or your partner already has a job that will keep you both for a while – then you might wish to forge your own path.

Otherwise, the question is, "Should I use a recruitment agency?" And the answer is yes and no. The right one will be your best ally, and the wrong one will crash your career faster than Richard Hammond on a bad day.

So, why would you use a recruitment agency instead of working alone?

The short answer is they're being paid by the potential employer. If they balls it up, they won't get paid, and they definitely will not get any repeat business in future. That means they're looking for the best fit for the company and the role in every sense. Including culture and mindset as well as skills and qualifications. They have to get it right.

Recruiters, on the whole, earn a fairly basic salary, and this is topped up with commission when they fill a vacancy. The industry is designed this way to keep them hungry and motivated. It's a sales job, and you're the commodity.

Like all industries, there are good and bad ones. The good ones really understand their client company, what it is they do, how their culture operates and what kind of person would fit in. In all likelihood they used to work in this industry prior to becoming a professional recruiter.

The bad ones apply the 'throw enough mud at the wall, and some of it will stick' mentality. You are the mud in that analogy! These are like the guys in a nightclub that keep asking women to sleep with them, if they ask 100, one of them will say yes.

But before you laugh, you need to put some work in too; you need to be nice and ensure that you're on the correct side of irritating. Don't be the guy who sends in your CV to dozens of agencies and waits for the recruiter to do all the work. That's what thousands of job hunters do, and then wonder why they don't hear back from recruiters!

On the other hand, don't be the guy who phones twice a day and gives them the hairdryer treatment when you don't have your dream job inside a week. They're not working for YOU, remember? I hate to break it to you, but you're just a piece of equipment to help them do their job. The successful candidate gets them paid, which might be someone else, so stay professional.

That doesn't mean they don't care about you – they do – but just as, say, a writer wants the best and most reliable laptop with the best and most reliable internet connection, your recruiter wants the best and most reliable candidate. That's you. So don't be that guy they dread calling.

How often is just right? You might have to take the cue from your recruiter, but agree upfront with them to make a regular slot to phone in and stick to it. Better still, offer value – at best, be proactive about your job hunt, and at the very least, be the person they don't dread talking to.

So how to tell if they are a good recruiter? What should you ask them?

How many people in the organisation have you met?
The rule of thumb in a larger organisation (150+) is that you need to have a relationship with at least 12 people to fully understand the culture.

Have you ever worked in the industry that you have recruited for?

Some will and some won't. Those that have will use the jargon in the correct context, those who haven't and are cuffing it, or are rubbish, will say all the right words and latest jargon but won't know what it means. When they tell you that the client is dynamic, ask them why and what does that mean? These guys need to fill vacancies, so they will use language similar to estate agents. Every client is prestigious, world-class, dynamic etc. Ask them why?

Advantages of Using a Recruiter

Recruiters get to hear about lots of jobs that might never hit the press or job boards. So, find a few you like and have a monthly call with them. Take them for a coffee. Invest in them, and they will invest in you. You want to be at the front of their mind. Once they get you a job, you go from candidate to hiring manager (i.e. their next client).

They don't – or shouldn't – cost you a penny. If they do, walk away.

They specialise where you're looking, and should know the market inside out. Just Google the industry news for that day and when you call one ask for their opinion on what's big in the news. You will soon find out the calibre of whom you're dealing with. Remember, this person will be representing you, so pick wisely.

They also offer other services in addition. If you're interview-shy, or just want someone to look over your CV (but not write it for you), this can be valuable.

And your part should be to:
- Be firm, fair and friendly with them. They are trying to earn a living in a highly competitive market where prices are being driven down; many see them as used car salesmen. Be nice and invest in the ones that you like.
- Be as flexible as you can. Most interviews are going to be during working hours, so even if you're in a temporary or contract job, make sure you'll be able to get to these.
- Listen carefully to any and all advice from your recruitment agency (but feel free to quietly pick and choose from within that).

For the recruiter, there will be many similarities between placing you and placing a new graduate. The advantage you have, however, is the life experience even the most well-drilled civilian candidate doesn't have. You're a problem solver, and that's your unique selling point.

The more they know about you, the better they can sell you to prospective companies. The more they know you, the more comfortable they will be in introducing you to their network. This is gold dust.

And recruiters don't just have access to candidates fresh to the market either, which brings us onto the subject of Headhunters. And if you don't think you have the kind of skills that fit a more specialist corner of the market...well, read on.

What are Headhunters Looking For?

In short, they're tasked with finding a specific skill set – and often a specific mindset – for a post. On rare occasions, Headhunters are supplied with a list of names that a company is keen to call in for an interview. These are candidates already doing this job well in a company that is often in competition with the Headhunter's client.

They could be individuals who have already made a splash within a particular industry, or they could be entrepreneurs who have a profile for a specific sector which a company might be keen to entice on board. The Headhunter's target is usually a very senior prospect, but they might also be a specific prospect, as mentioned above; a former Forces candidate, for example.

Headhunters usually advertise themselves as 'executive search organisations', but don't let that put you off. Is it worth you approaching them? Absolutely yes. But only if, to coin a cliché, you have all your ducks in a row. These guys can seriously help you grow your network and market you as a brand if done correctly. Ask them about local networking events and places where you can meet the movers and shakers in the industry you want to get into. Go along with your CV on nice paper and meet people, tell them about your 'why', ask for advice on your CV (do not say 'Giz a Job'!)

A senior or specific appointment means a hefty bonus to a recruiter, so why wouldn't they want to hear from you? They normally get paid a fee of between 20 and 30% value of your annual salary.

A Word of Warning

We've talked about the good, but the bad and the ugly are out there too. If a recruitment agency is asking you for money, you have to wonder what the hell they're doing for their clients. Also, what are they offering for it? If you're given a lot of platitudes about interview training and CV help, well, a lot of good companies will do that absolutely for free, as building a good name within the industry with the best candidates makes this an excellent investment.

If they do plan to charge you, they have to make this clear up front, and you need to agree to the service. If a mysterious bill comes out of nowhere, tell them where to go, or get in touch with me on my website and I will happily have a look at the circumstances for you (at £50 per hour!). Only joking, time allowing, I will happily look into it for free since you have invested in my book.

Warning bells should ring if:
- You are asked for money, especially for services which should be standard with a recruiter. Google what's out there or ask your Accountability Group.
- You find bad reviews online. Bear in mind you may get the odd disgruntled candidate (often you can tell exactly why they've had trouble getting a job from their feedback!). But when everyone seems to be telling the same story, listen to them.

Additionally, as previously mentioned, you don't need someone to write your CV for you. Getting someone else to look over it and advise you on it is another matter, but it has to sound like you. There are legitimate 'career counsellors' out there, and you might feel that you'd benefit from working with one in due course, so don't confuse these with the cowboys that take your money to find you a job.

Temping Agencies & How to Find One

If you haven't got a buffer, and you need to find work, any work right now, you need to find a reputable temping agency right away. You could find yourself doing almost anything, as they're not just for secretarial work. It's not likely to be very interesting, or very lucrative, but as we've said already if you need money, that £10-£12 per hour is a lot better than £0 per hour, especially if you have debts that need to be chipped away at.

Temp jobs are also easy to give notice on if the right job comes along, so you're not trapped in a dead-end gig, watching other opportunities pass you by. As a means for bypassing taking just 'any' job, it's a no-brainer.

What to Look for in a Temping Agency

- Avoid anyone asking you for money – that's not an agency, that's an extortion racket.
- Go for the big names (i.e. Reed, Adecco, Manpower, etc.) to have a

steady stream of work in a variety of sectors.
- Take online reviews with a pinch of salt – but don't entirely disregard them if they all relate to one particular branch.

Smaller agencies can often negotiate better rates (although they tend to have fewer opportunities). There's no limit to how many you can sign up for, so this is one of the few times where a scattergun approach can work.

You might want a separate email address for your temping exploits – nothing fills up an inbox like temp agency mail, and you don't want to miss that important email from a recruiter by weeding through the chaff.

If your temping agency is offering free skills training, take advantage of it, even if you don't think you'll need it. Being able to touch type quickly saves hours out of anyone's working week.

Use temping for your own ends. If you want to work somewhere in particular, and the company has a reputation for weighting their recruitment towards internal hires, find out who has their temporary worker contract and get yourself placed there. It doesn't matter if you're there to sort the post; if you demonstrate you're "not our usual temp", you're in the door.

LinkedIn and Networking

LinkedIn is a great tool to make a reputation for yourself. Ensure you have a profile and that it mirrors your CV.

Make it tangible and make sure that your profile passes the '10 second' test. Prospective recruiters, Headhunters, and employers need to get what you offer in under 10 seconds. If they do, they will call for a chat.

Use a professional photo. If you want to be a builder, make sure you're wearing clean builder-type attire in your picture. If you want to be a bank manager, don't have a picture of you in your ceremonial gear stood outside Buckingham Palace. Or even worse, a picture of you streaking at the Army vs Navy at Twickenham! Hilarious, but erm…no!

Be active. Ask questions, write a blog on your chosen career (up to 600 words) and make it engaging. Start your blog with a question that piques interest and always add an image to the post. No, your streaking picture will not suffice.

Love the critics and the haters too. Not everyone will like you or relate to you. Some will be critical of what you write, and this is excellent. Why?

Because it tells you something that you can improve on. It's those people that read your stuff and never comment. They leave you in the dark.

Praise is nice, but critics are better. They give shape to your next blog or piece of content you are going to post online. My rule of thumb is never write anything that your mum would be upset by, and that when you are rich and famous won't come back to bite you! You have been warned.

THIS CHAPTER IN A NUTSHELL

Your Plan of Action

- Register with appropriate recruiters for your chosen industry.
- Consider approaching a Headhunter, particularly one with a track-record of placing people in the industry you want to get into, they can help you network.
- Research your industry news and form some questions to ask recruiters. The good ones will remember you as someone who has their finger on the pulse. The bad ones will know that you know they're winging it. If you sound like a credible, well-read candidate, they will be queueing up to put you in front of good clients.
- Ask recruiters and Headhunters if they know of any good local opportunities to network. Go along, talk about your 'why', take your CV, ask for advice on it and press the flesh.
- Write a blog on LinkedIn; ask questions in forums regarding the industry you want to join. Contribute and grow your network.
- If you need to earn money now, register with at least three temping agencies.

Things to Note

- You won't find a job overnight – stay focused, and check in with your Accountability Group of friends and family.
- Discuss whether you can wait for 'the job', or whether you need to take 'any job' (or temp) for the sake of the family's finances.
- IF A RECRUITER IS ASKING YOU FOR MONEY, IT'S A SCAM. That needed to be in capital letters. If you're not familiar with how civilian working life operates, it's easy to be sucked in.

6 YOU AS A BRAND

Setting up my own brand was done in my last year in the military. I registered www.chrishitchens.co.uk using LCN.com and hosted a small HTML website with my CV and a picture of myself that couldn't be any cheesier if it was sponsored by dairylea.

I set myself up on LinkedIn and put my CV in front of anyone in a suit to ask for advice. I would go to networking events; I would go to anything where it involved cutting a ribbon to network, even if it was opening the local supermarket. I would be there with my CV in hand to ask for advice. The great thing was I was honing my skills, my handshake, watching how people reacted. It allowed me to try different elevator pitches about myself to see how they reacted. All the time I was sharpening my brand.

That sounds like the worst kind of marketing-speak, doesn't it? We have spoken about LinkedIn briefly, but what about the other lines of communication? Let's immediately get over the bit where your skin is crawling at the prospect, and you are ready to run the other way!

At the end of the day, your reputation, your CV, everything about you that's online, is a *product*. It should be working hard for you and opening the doors to opportunity for you. This is especially important if you have had a good think about entering the job hunting market, and you know you could make a go of it by setting up in business by yourself instead.

Why is this important? Because if you're selling a product or service, and certainly as a one-man (or woman) band, you're also selling *you* and it has to be worth what your asking price is. And to put a word of warning in here at the start, setting up on your own is hard. It can affect your family time, both in terms of you being either physically or emotionally absent, and it can also be financially tough – trust me on this. Ever heard the saying, it takes at least 10 years of hard graft to make an overnight success?

You might even like to get a job – any job – to alleviate that financial worry, and work on your own business as a side-project for a year before you fully launch. Clients breed clients, especially if you have good reviews, so launching with only 50% of what you need plus a financial buffer is enough to give you a sound start.

So, onto branding you.

Where to Start

With the basics – your 'why' of course. Beyond that: clean, sober, presentable – are obvious, unless you are going into stand-up comedy or politics. But if you're self-employed, you kind of have to live the job, all day, every day, and certainly to start with, you might feel that you're always "on". That might well be the case at first, but it will – if you put the work in – be worth it in the end.

Think of a popular product, a household name – perhaps a certain electronics brand whose logo is a piece of fruit with a bite taken out of it. What is that household name selling you, even over and above the product? They're selling you a guarantee – everything we do 'just works', 'we think differently', 'we like to innovate' etc.

They are selling you their 'why'. The fact that it's a piece of gorgeously designed electronics is almost irrelevant. You're buying their 'why'. That's what you need to do too.

What Will Happen if I Don't Work on My Brand?

You might do okay. You might even make a reasonable living. But you will have to work harder to differentiate yourself from the competition and to get clients. You will probably find that you're having to undercut the competition to get the jobs too, rather than allowing your skills and abilities – your brand - to set your prices for you.

In short, not getting your personal brand (and we're back to your 'why' here) right means that you're working harder, and working longer hours, for less money. None of that adds up to a bright future outside of the military for you or your family.

Remember, clients want to know what's in it for them. Not you. Getting your brand and message right gets you labelled as a key person of influence. It makes you stand out, and when you are a 'KPI', opportunities come to you.

Take my situation as an example. Because of the people I've helped get jobs in the last decade, I often get asked to publicly speak about the subjects in this book. I am classed as a key person of influence when it comes to getting people jobs that they really want. My brand is something that I am always working on. I suggest you do too.

What Will Happen if I Do Work on My Brand?
You'll be putting your personal 'why' into practice every day of your working life. And if you've really done your homework and found the intersection of what you love doing, what you're good at, and what people will pay you to do, well… the old adage about loving what you do means you never do a day's work in your life isn't strictly true, but it does make a hell of a difference on difficult days when your clients got out of bed on the wrong side, and your main supplier sent the wrong order.

You will become a key person of influence in your niche of your industry. Opportunities will come to you. People will ask you before going to the market to recruit.

But just saying "great, let's go for it – I'll be a genuine and authentic version of me so that my clients get exactly what they see, with the guarantee of my ex-military honest and loyalty" isn't quite enough. You need to refine that for civilian life.

Here's your first bit of homework:
Decide what you're doing – really decide what you're doing – your proposition has to be clear. And your pitch has to be razor sharp. In no more than 60 seconds you need to be able to articulate what it is you do. You need to be able to fix a problem that others are willing to pay for and it always needs to be evolving to stay ahead of the competition. Nobody buys things that will make their life worse; only things they believe will make their life better.

What makes you different? How are you changing the market and evolving a service that is already out there? Interestingly, about 20 years ago, Kodak said that digital photography would never take off. That ended well. Waterstones spent a fortune on shops – Amazon brought out the Kindle. It's hard work making money from your own business, so test your ideas with your Accountability Group before diving in and dressed like something on Dragon's Den.

Publish. Yep, write blogs, ask questions on LinkedIn, get your name out there and get people talking. It's free to do and people who are interested will engage. The key people of influence in your industry will be interested in meeting this new person who has a voice. You can learn a lot from them. So keep publishing. Once a week if you can, or at least once a month.

Let's say you're going to use all your former Forces skills, and set up as a life coach for others either leaving the military or re-joining the workforce after a long break. That's your niche; the thing you're good at, the thing you enjoy doing (because who doesn't enjoy helping others get on the right track too?), and the thing that people will pay you for. And your unique selling point? There's not much out there to help former military personnel. Except now there's you too.

Remember the exercise in Chapter One? Can you monetise this? Is it scalable? Will it provide passive income, or will you have to personally chisel out every single pound coin with hard graft?

Do your homework. You can't copy someone else's brand, or someone else's 'why'. But you can read up on those that have built themselves up from – in many cases – absolutely nothing into successful businesspeople. Bear in mind that here, as with any other area of your life, you'll have to make your own mistakes, but you can certainly make those mistakes less costly by studying the efforts of others.

Study your competitors. Who else is out there doing what you're planning to do? How are they doing it? How successful are they, and what's their background? How do people speak about their brand (and is it how you'd like people to speak about yours)? What mistakes are they making – or what are they doing right – that will translate to your business?

How much work do you need to do on you? This is where your support network can help. If your head still hasn't left the military, then you might have more work to do before you can launch yourself. You might even find that you need to take a job – any job – first, to put a break between your life before, and yourself and your new business now.

Don't go and spend thousands on a website. Build a landing page using something like WordPress and market it on social media to test interest. If there is no interest, play around with the description of what it is you're offering. Connect with your audience using blogs that ask questions and bring to life the problem you are trying to solve. Go find a really good digital marketer on www.PeoplePerHour.co.uk and ask for help.

Once you have tested your idea and there is a demand, you can then work out how much you want to invest. Business is about turning £1 into £2. As an investor, if a business can show me that for every £1 they spend at the front of the business, it equates to £2 at the till, I'm in. A lot of new entrepreneurs get blinkered by their product and kind of forget that the business needs to make a profit. If it doesn't, you're not running a business, you're running a charity.

Get a good accountant and bookkeeper. Go and see at least three accountants and tell them that you want an 'all in bill' for doing the books, giving you a monthly breakdown, doing your VAT (if applicable), your annual reporting to HMRC and Companies House, all of your personal tax and that you want to be able to ask questions without getting charged.

Accountants are there to make money, they are a business just like you. And they're not your friend, they're your business partner. If you don't agree on things up front, then expect the invoices to come in thick and fast. The same goes for Lawyers. If you need one, go see three and make it clear that you do not want ever increasing invoices coming in that you didn't plan for.

Practical Tax Stuff: The Tax Man
Think of the tax man as your friend. No, seriously. Seeing the tax man as your enemy is a poor start, as HMRC can actually be a great source of help and advice and assist you in starting your own business. You need to tell the tax man when you start working for yourself. The website www.hmrc.gov.uk will give you all the helpful information you need on what records you need to keep, as well as information on filling in and filing a tax return (helpful hint – unless you're very organised and very good with numbers, get an accountant to do this for you).

Other useful official sources of information for the newly self-employed include Money Advice Service – www.moneyadviceservice.org.uk, and the Citizens' Advice Bureau – www.citizensadvice.org.uk.

Expenses and Record Keeping
What you can claim for will depend on the nature of your business, but in short, you need to keep:

• Receipts for any purchases made solely for your business

- Receipts for any travel carried out solely for your business
- Copies of any orders (online is fine)
- Copies of any invoices (again, online is fine), both from you to your clients and from suppliers to you

If your accounts are reasonably straightforward, and you're okay with numbers or have an accountant in the family that's still on your Christmas card list, you might want to use software like TaxCalc (www.taxcalc.com) and complete your own tax return. It presents you with a simplified form to fill in and populates the longer document for you. Services like FreeAgent (www.freeagent.com) are also very useful regarding keeping your own basic accounts.

However, I can't say it enough – if you're not great with numbers (and even if you are), find an accountant. It will save you money in the long run.

Social Media

If you're going to set up on your own, social media can be one of the most effective ways of engaging with new customers, and also one of the biggest pitfalls. If you're inclined to use social media for expressing personal or political views (no matter how mainstream or inoffensive), you need to separate your business pages from your personal ones and be careful not to confuse the two.

If you can't trust yourself to do this – or you're worried you might forget what you're posting where – invest the money in getting a social media manager to run your accounts for you. It's not a waste of money if it's going to stop you making a massive faux pas. It's not just for status updates either; engage customers with video, photographs, and longer blog style posts.

At the very least, use Facebook and Twitter for your business, LinkedIn if you're looking to network within your industry and perhaps maintain that all-important industry-related blog, and if there's any kind of pictorial element to your business, Pinterest, Instagram, and YouTube too.

If that seems like a full-time job in itself, you're not wrong. There are programs and apps that schedule social media posts, but being responsive to clients is important. Again, if you feel this will detract from getting on with the job, get a social media manager on it; there are Virtual Assistants who will take on and manage the accounts of several businesses every single day who can keep on top of your social media business while you're taking care of actual business.

I cannot stress this next part enough. Make your content interesting. You can populate your Facebook business page daily, but if it's boring, no one is going to interact with it. Here are some tips:

- Make sure you are talking about your 'why' and make it original.
- Quirky sayings, clichés and sound bites from other people are just boring. It isn't content, and it isn't you. It basically tells me you have nothing original to say.
- Plagiarise, but adapt it to your 'why'. Regurgitate, hell no. I am not interested in your favourite Winston Churchill quote. I am interested *why* it's your favourite and what you plan on doing because of it.
- Don't make it wall to wall sales – share fun stuff relevant to your business, and use social media to build your brand as a friendly and approachable expert.
- Even if you employ a social media manager, dedicate five minutes a day (or half an hour a week) to engaging with your pages yourself – perhaps details of your working week, or news about your business. Make it original and about you.
- Don't forget to thank new followers – it's the first point of engagement and could lead to a customer.
- Add social media icons to your website so your customers can find you easily.

Bad Feedback

I remember being in a briefing once and when the nervous young officer had finished running through his plan, the boss politely pointed out his shortcomings culminating with, "I am afraid you cannot polish this turd Mr Smith…"

The room fell silent, and we could toast marshmallows from his face it was that red. Feeling his pain and obviously feeling quite charitable, one of the old and bold pilots hilariously chipped in with, "But you can roll it in glitter sir."

When you go public on social media, sell a service, or even if you're ever silly enough to bear your soul and write a book, you will always get feedback - good and bad. Unfortunately, sometimes there is never enough glitter around when you need it most.

The key is to always be polite and respectful, and where appropriate, outline the circumstances of what has led to the feedback or complaint for others to see. In other words, use your natural integrity to make even a foul up a positive learning experience. Acknowledge your shortcomings and show that you are capable of learning and putting this right. If the cap fits and all that.

A bad customer experience handled well can be as useful regarding building your business as a good one. If the customer is determined to be rude and abusive, don't engage like for like. Suggest that they can message you privately, or talk to you on the phone instead.

If you do a good job, your customers will tell 5 people. If you do a bad job, they will tell 15.

Your Company Website

So, the landing pages have taken off, you have an audience on social media and people want to know more. Unless you're planning to build your customer base entirely from your social media accounts, you will need at the very least a basic website to let people know who you are and what you do. Unless you're a skilled web designer, you might want to get a freelancer to do this for you.

My pet hate is people build websites because they think they just need a website, without clarifying what it's actual purpose is. Why do you need a website? What is it going to do for you, and for your clients?

You can buy domain names very reasonably from a variety of companies, and some even offer add-ons like simple templates to get you up and running, like www.LCN.co.uk.

What Should Go on My Website?

It can be as basic as you like at first – perhaps nothing more than a brief outline of your skills and services, and a contact page. Again, the more complex your business (and your website), the more you'd be best advised to get a professional to set it up for you.

A Word on Freelancers and Freelance Sites

Just as with the rest of the world, there are some great freelancers and some not so great freelancers out there. You can't be an expert at everything, and farming out some of the work to people who are great gives you time to actually work on your business, or even more importantly, have a few hours in the day to spend with the family.

A few pointers:
- Ask to see examples of previous work before you agree to work with

someone.

- Be wary of freelancers quoting very low prices – at best it indicates a lack of experience and desperation for work, and at worst, it indicates that they're sub-contracting to other workers outside the UK whose work you won't have seen.
- Freelancers often know other good and reliable freelancers – if you need other skills and don't want to start your search from scratch, ask people you've worked with before who they would recommend.

In terms of finding experienced and talented freelancers, try sites like www.peopleperhour.com. Their responsive customer service makes them a good bet for client and freelancer alike. Plus, you have the peace of mind of reading their client feedback before selecting your freelancer.

THIS CHAPTER IN A NUTSHELL

Your Plan of Action
- Network, get out and meet people and learn what works and what doesn't.
- Use what you learn to sort out your pitch. Ensure that your proposition fixes a problem and offers value.
- Some things will go wrong, learn from them and adjust what you need to.
- Publish. Get your voice out there. At least once a month.
- Try and identify the Key People of Influence in your industry. Follow them, learn from them.
- Contact HMRC and register as self-employed.
- Do not spend a penny unless your idea is proved that it can turn £1 into £2.
- Test your ideas with your Accountability Group and anyone else before spending a penny.
- Set up (or at least reserve) your social media accounts for your business.
- Buy the domain names for your business (even if you don't do anything with them just yet).
- If you are going to use Social Media, do not just regurgitate another people's content. Sell your 'why'.

Things to Note
- You can't be an expert at everything – whether it's branding you, or branding your business, find other experts to work with you.
- Keep business and social life separate – if you know you're likely to take your personal life into your business social media accounts, get a social media manager to run them for you.

A FINAL WORD

Congratulations! You made it to the end of the book, which I hope is the first of many future achievements. I hope you now feel you have at least a few tools to help you make your transition out of the military and into civilian life.

I'll expand on a lot of the chapters both on www.leavingthemilitary.co.uk and in further books and web content to keep things up to date and relevant to the changing job market.

You can also message me on the website to let me know which bits of the book worked, and which bits I need to improve on! My 'why' is all about hearing what you learnt and how you succeeded, so please get in touch. Also, on the website you will find useful spreadsheets and worksheets to save you a lot of time.

Use your Accountability Group and remember to give yourself a break. The world moves slower than you think, so manage your expectations accordingly. Things take six times longer than you think. That's right, not twice as slowly, but at least six times slower. Deep down no one wants to believe that (even me), but that's the way it is sometimes. A watched pot never boils! So, patience is the name of the game.

No one can quite "know how you feel", not even if they've followed a similar path to you. Everyone's experiences are different, and although they can know what you might be experiencing, your feelings are your feelings. As for getting over it, you might never entirely "get over it", but your experiences both in the military and quitting the military will give you tools to build the next stage of your life and your career.

I'll say it again, if you find that you're not coping, and it's affecting your family as well as you, seek help. There are web links throughout this book for help organisations and grouped together in the helpful appendix at the end.

If you – or by default, your family – are in crisis at any point, particularly if you feel suicidal, or cannot see any other way out of your current situation, please call the Samaritans on 116 123 (UK). It's free, and you will be listened to in a non-judgemental and supportive way. It's often easier to talk to a stranger than it is your own support network. If you don't feel you can talk, email at jo@samaritans.org, or visit the website www.samaritans.org to find your local branch office.

There is life after the military. You might not want to be here, you might never have expected to be here – even if it's your own choice to leave – but you have been shaped into who you are by the Forces. Take that into the civilian world, and build a great career and life for you and your family.

The very best of luck and I hope to hear that my book has helped in some small way. Please feel free to get in touch and let me know your thoughts. Good or bad!

As we used to say, "May you have as many landings as take off's!"

Kind regards

Chris

ALL THE WEBSITES, ALL IN ONE PLACE

www.leavingthemilitary.co.uk – website for this book and source of worksheets and other downloads which will help you plan your strategy. Also, discussion forums where you can talk to other people about your journey.

Money
www.moneysavingexpert.com – a brilliant source of advice that does exactly what it says on the tin. Also, useful (if occasionally boisterous) forums where you can ask for advice.

www.moneyadviceservice.org.uk – connected to the financial regulator, and therefore a sound and accurate source of advice on anything from household budgeting to pensions.

www.stepchange.org – if you're in debt, contact them now. That's NOW. Before you do anything else. Get your repayment schedule in place, and stop losing sleep over what you owe.

Self-help and addiction
www.alcoholics-anonymous.org.uk – self-explanatory; if you're not using alcohol sensibly, or have had trouble in the past, and you're worried that a major life change will tip you over the edge again, get in touch with the AA. They're not just there for you, but for your family as well.

www.adfam.org.uk – a brilliant addiction organisation who are geared towards supporting the addict's family. Addiction can be lonely for everyone involved.

www.mind.org.uk – if you're struggling at all with leaving the military and feel you'd like to talk to someone about your mental health in a professional capacity, do so. Seeking help is not weak; it's strong, and it's brave.

Self-employment

www.hmrc.gov.uk – essential if you're thinking of becoming self-employed, and your source for any kind of applications for credits and queries about tax.

www.citizensadvice.org.uk – a one-stop shop for all kinds of impartial consumer and workplace advice.

www.taxcalc.com – software which will make filing your tax return online an absolute doddle (providing you've got all your paperwork and login details to hand!).

www.freeagent.com – a great web-based subscription service for keeping your self-employed accounts in order.

www.LCN.co.uk – one of many domain name providers, but one of the best regarding providing you with an easy, intuitive control panel, plus the option to build your own simple website with free templates.

www.peopleperhour.com – a source of some of the finest curated freelance talent in the world, graded by (site) experience level, feedback, and client review. You might even want to dip your own toe in if your skills are rarer and command a high fee.

Jobs

www.glassdoor.co.uk – A really good website for looking at anonymous company reviews. Take them with a pinch of salt, but they can help you understand the values and culture of a prospective company.

www.linkedin.com – A professional social media site. Great for asking questions and posting blogs to get you noticed.

Suggested Reading

Simon Sinek - Start With Why: How Great Leaders Inspire Everyone To Take Action

Simon Sinek - Leaders Eat Last: Why Some Teams Pull Together and Others Don't

Napoleon Hill - Think and Grow Rich

ABOUT THE AUTHOR

I grew up in Leyland, Lancashire and was the middle of three boys. I went to a convent Junior School, which probably explains my warped sense of humour and many character flaws. After the Convent, I went on to study at the local high school, and after 5 years of torturing the poor teachers I went on to study Engineering after a brief encounter with hairdressing. Yes, really.

On a very rare day off I visited the Army career's office with a close friend who was joining up. I was confronted with a Warrant Officer who asked if I wanted to have a go at the entrance exam. Politely declining, the Warrant Officer then asked me if I was too scared to take the test. It was at this point a career was born. Well, kind of...

I was informed I had the aptitude to become a pilot, but not the exam grades so I would have to start as an Airtrooper (great sales technique from the careers office by the way!). But not one to back away from a challenge, I said I was committed to joining and went home to tell my Mum and Dad who were speechless. The dog was also sad and didn't acknowledge me for some time afterwards. My brothers were delighted at the new real estate that was coming onto the market (my bedroom), and that was me, I was off.

So, I joined the Army Air Corps in 1989 and went on to 656 Squadron where I became the Squadron Physical Training Instructor. I started at night school to attain the grades needed to become a pilot. From there I went to Northern Ireland as a door gunner and then into the Ops room where I successfully completed my pilot selection and was subsequently awarded a place on the pilot's course.

On passing the course (which deserves a book in its own right), I was posted to Germany and was then posted to Cyprus for 3 years. In Cyprus, I decided to live outside of the barracks in a local village. There, I was lucky enough to rub shoulders with hedge fund managers and other senior financial services people and a new seed was planted.

The Army in its wisdom posted me back to Northern Ireland, but at this point, I had decided that I had achieved everything I wanted and decided to leave the military. I was posted back to Middle Wallop for my final year where I spent every penny on courses and getting myself ready for my own transition.

My transition was a rocky one, and after getting fired from my first job, I went into project management within one of the large consultancies, learnt my trade and met some brilliant people. After which, I set myself up as a contractor, managing projects and programmes up to £97M and with over 450 people all over the world.

In 2010, I set up my first proper limited company employing people, which had three divisions and a subsidiary software company. The purpose of the company was to provide consultancy, due diligence services, and experts to the wealth management sector.

The company was the first in the UK to get Investors in People Gold and ISO:9001 together on the first attempt and broke its first million within 9 months of operation. It went on to become a multi-million-pound company as did the software company. Me and my Financial Director (the long-suffering Roger, who must get a mention) took the business to Cranfield Management School where the business won the premier business award, beating 40 other businesses.

An American company came calling to buy the subsidiary software company, but the original company nose-dived, ceased trading and went into administration due to a change in regulations affecting its customers and our market. So, we had to shut the business down. It wasn't pretty and was quite an emotional and painful rollercoaster. But we all learned a lot, some of it the hard way! But luckily, one business was sold.

Due to a wife and two boisterous young boys (who I have decided take after their Mother...), I decided to go back into Project Management as a contractor to keep my sanity, and I have since started a few other businesses helping other entrepreneurs realise their goals.

It was here I came into contact with service leavers who literally had no idea how to get a job and the life they were capable of, so I decided to share my experiences. Since then I have spoken at many events on how to get a job and have run workshops to help people get the life they want after the forces. It was the feedback from these events that gave me the motivation for this book and the others I have planned. I am passionate about seeing service leavers do well. That is my 'why'.

What little spare time I have is devoted to my family, and managing the www.AACHonourroll.com and the associated Facebook group.

I hope you enjoyed my book and if I can improve it in any way, then let me know. If you have time to leave me a message on www.leavingthemilitary.co.uk I will do my best to respond.

All the best for the future,

Chris

33182119R00049

Printed in Poland
by Amazon Fulfillment
Poland Sp. z o.o., Wrocław